IELTS Testbuilder 2

Sam McCarter

MACMILLAN

Macmillan Education
Between Towns Road, Oxford OX4 3PP
A division of Macmillan Publishers Limited
Companies and representatives throughout the world

ISBN 978-0-230-02883-8

Text © Sam McCarter 2008
Design and illustration © Macmillan Publishers Limited 2008

First published 2008

Designed by eMC Design Ltd, www.emcdesign.org.uk
Illustrated by eMC Design Ltd, Martin Sanders
Cover design by Macmillan Publishers Limited
Cover photograph by Image Source

Authors' acknowledgements
I would like to thank Micky Silver for the article on left-handedness p78 and Wendy Riley
for Physician, Rule Thyself! p83. I would also like to say a special thank you to Xanthe Sturt
Taylor for her patience. I would also like to thank the following students for the writing
samples: Bassam Khalil, Abdulkadir Hadi, Luse Kanumuangi, Abukar Haji Jimale, Wilonja
Mutebwe.

The publishers would like to thank Liz Hunt and Edward Lee for their help.

The author and publishers would like to thank the following for permission to reproduce
their photographs: Alamy / John Arnold Images p102, Alamy / Jenny Hart p21, Alamy /
David Wall p72; Corbis / Edward Block p54 Corbis / Horace Bristol p44, Corbis / James
Richardson pp112, 113; Getty / Superstudio p16.

The author(s) and publishers are grateful for permission to reprint the following copyright
material: Australian Academy of Technological Sciences and Engineering (ATSE) for the
diagram "Water recycling in Australia" published on www.atse.org.au © ATSE 2004 p87;
The Economist for an extract from "Much ado about almost nothing" published in The
Economist 18th March 2004 © The Economist Newspaper Limited, London 2004 p112;
Extract from "History of Blue Plaques Scheme 2" published on www.english-heritage.
org.uk, © Emily Cole used by permission of the author p102; Professor Michael D.
Guiry, Martin Ryan Institute for extracts from www.seaweed.ie p44; Office for National
Statistics for the diagrams "Transport Highlights, Passenger railway journeys, GB" p30
and "Working Lives: Half of women's jobs are part time – All in employment: by sex
and occupation, 2005, UK" p115 © Crown copyright, and facts from "Participation: More
volunteers from higher income homes" from the Home Office Citizenship Survey, 2001 p27
© Crown copyright, all published on www.statistics.gov.uk; Te Ara, Encyclopedia of New
Zealand for information about caves by Leslie Owen Kermode, B.A., Geological Survey
Station, Department of Scientific and Industrial Research, Otahuhu published on www.
teara.govt.nz p72; Cambridge ESOL for an extract adapted from IELTS Practice Materials
and candidates Booklet © 2006 p7.

Printed and bound in Thailand

2014 2013 2012 2011 2010
8   7   6   5   4

CONTENTS

IELTS Testbuilder 2

The IELTS Testbuilder 2 is more than a book of Practice Tests. It is designed not only to enable students to practise doing tests of exactly the kind they will encounter in the exam itself, but also to provide them with valuable further practice, guidance and explanation. This will enable them to prepare thoroughly for the exam and increase their ability to perform well. IELTS Testbuilder 2 has been developed for **all** students preparing for the academic component of the IELTS examination. Students who are at Band 4.5 will find the book as useful as those who are aiming for Band 6 and above.

The IELTS Testbuilder 2 contains:

Four complete Practice Tests for the academic version of the International English Language Testing System

These tests closely reflect the level and types of question to be found in the exam.

Further Practice and Guidance pages

In each test, these follow each paper or section of a paper.

In the READING AND LISTENING TESTS, there are exercises, questions, advice and tips directly related to each paper or section. These encourage students to reach their own decisions as to what the answers in the tests should be. Their step-by-step approach enables students to develop and apply the appropriate processes when answering the questions in the exam.

In the WRITING TEST, there are language development exercises which help with planning, and a range of authentic sample answers for the student to assess.

In the SPEAKING TEST, there are examples of possible question areas, guidance in topic development and suggestions for useful language.

Key and Explanation

This contains full explanations of answers in the Tests and Further Practice pages. For headings, multiple-choice and True/False/Not Given and Yes/No/Not Given questions etc., there are clear and detailed explanations not only of the correct answer, but also of why the other options are incorrect.

How to use the IELTS Testbuilder 2

1   Simply follow the instructions page by page. Clear directions are given as to the order in which to do things. If you follow this order, you:

- complete one part of a paper, perhaps under exam conditions, and then

either

- do the Further Practice and Guidance pages relating to that part. You then check the answers to the questions in those pages and review the answers given to the questions in the test in the light of what has been learnt from doing the Further Practice and Guidance pages. After that, you can check the answers to the questions in the test and go through the explanations.

or

- check the answers to the questions in the test and go through the explanations if there are no Further Practice and Guidance pages and

then

- move on to the next part of the test.

2   Vary the order.

You may wish to do some of the Further Practice and Guidance pages before answering the questions in the test that they relate to.

Note to teachers

As an alternative to the above, you may wish to do the Further Practice and Guidance pages as discussion or pairwork, or ask students to prepare them before class.

The International English Language Testing System

The following is a brief summary of what the exam consists of. Additional details of what is tested in each Paper are given in the relevant Further Practice and Guidance pages.

The Listening Module   approximately 30 minutes

Contents	Situations	Question Type
There are four separate sections which you hear only once. There are usually 40 questions. You have time to read the questions and time at the end to transfer your answers to the answer sheet. As the test progresses, the difficulty of the questions, tasks and text increases.	The first two sections are of a general, social nature. There will be a conversation between two people and then usually a monologue or an interview. In the third and fourth sections, the contexts are of an educational or training nature. There will be a conversation of up to four speakers and then a talk/lecture of general academic interest.	The question types may include: • multiple-choice questions • sentence completion • short-answer questions • completion of tables/charts/summary/notes/flow-chart • labelling a diagram/plan/ map • classification • matching.

The Academic Reading Module   60 minutes

Contents	Texts	Question Type
There are three reading passages with a total of 1,500 to 2,500 words. There are 40 questions. You must write your answers on the answer sheet within the 60 minutes. As the test progresses, the difficulty of the questions, tasks and text increases.	The texts are of the type you find in magazines, journals, textbooks and newspapers. The topics are not specific to any one discipline. They are all accessible to candidates who are entering undergraduate or postgraduate courses. There is at least one article, which contains detailed logical argument.	The question types may include: • multiple-choice questions • sentence completion • short-answer questions • completion of tables/charts/summary/notes • choosing headings from a list • identification of a writer's views or attitudes (yes/no/not given) or identification of information in the passage (true/false/not given) • classification • matching lists • matching phrases • labelling a diagram.

The Academic Writing Module   60 minutes

There are two compulsory writing tasks.

Contents	Texts	Assessment Criteria
Task 1 You are advised to spend 20 minutes and write a minimum of 150 words.	You will be asked to describe a diagram or data i.e. a graph, table or chart.	You will be assessed on your ability to: • organize, present and compare data • answer the question which is asked • use English grammar and vocabulary • use language that is appropriate in style, register and content • write in a way that your reader can follow.
Task 2 You are advised to spend 40 minutes and write a minimum of 250 words.	You will be asked to express and justify your opinion of a point of view, problem etc. or to discuss a problem.	You will be assessed on your ability to: • write in an appropriate style • present a solution to the problem • present and justify your opinion • compare and contrast evidence and opinions • evaluate and challenge ideas.

The Speaking Module   11–14 minutes

Contents	Task Type	Assessment Criteria
There are three sections: Part 1 (4–5 minutes) Introduction and interview	The examiner will introduce himself/herself, check your identification and then ask you questions about yourself, your home, interests etc.	In all parts of the speaking module, you will be assessed on your: • fluency and coherence • vocabulary • grammatical range and accuracy • pronunciation.
Part 2 (3–4 minutes) Individual long turn	You will be given a card with a subject on which you will be asked to prepare a short talk of 1–2 minutes. You will be given pencil and paper to make notes.	
Part 3 (4–5 minutes) Two-way discussion	You will take part in a discussion with the examiner on a subject related to the one in Part 2.	

Completing the mark sheets   (please see pages 173–174)

Candidates

- may use upper or lower case in writing their answers.

- should take care when writing their answers on the Listening Answer Sheet as poor spelling and grammar are penalized.

- may use both UK and US varieties of spelling.

- should write only one answer for questions where the answer is a single letter or number. If more than one answer is written, the answer is marked wrong.

- will be penalized if they exceed the word limit. If a question specifies an answer using NO MORE THAN THREE WORDS and the correct answer is *black leather coat*, the answer *coat of black leather* is incorrect.

- should transfer only the necessary missing word(s) on to the Answer Sheet where they are expected to complete a gap. For example, if a candidate has to complete 'in the ....' and the correct answer is *morning* the answer *in the morning* would be incorrect.

- must transfer their answers on to the Answer Sheet within the time allocated in both Reading and Listening papers.

Results

For notes on how IELTS is scored, see page 175.

For further information about the exam see also the IELTS Handbook and www.IELTS.org.

Note that you will hear each section once only in the exam.

Before listening to the recording and completing Sections 1–2, go on to pages 11–12.

Section 1   Questions 1–10

Questions 1–4

Complete the notes below.

*Write **NO MORE THAN THREE WORDS AND/OR A NUMBER** for each answer.*

ITALIABREAKS

Example	Destination	..*Venice*..

Name	John	1 ....
Mobile number	07987	2 ....
Number of people	Two adults	
Holiday length		3 ....
Hotel Scotland		4 .... star

Questions 5 and 6

*Choose **TWO** letters A–E.*

*Which **TWO** good things about Hotel Scotland are mentioned?*

    A restaurant

    B convenience

    C room with a terrace

    D large rooms

    E cleanliness

Questions 7–10

Write **NO MORE THAN THREE WORDS AND/OR A NUMBER** *for each answer.*

7   The departure date is ....

8   The holiday excluding insurance costs £ ....

9   The discount is .... per cent if booked before 17th February.

10   The booking reference is ....

Stop the recording when you hear 'That is the end of Section 1'. Now check your answers.

Section 2   Questions 11–20

Questions 11–13

Write NO MORE THAN THREE WORDS for each answer.

11 The land for development has not been used for over a ....

12 There was pressure to build a training centre and a .... on the land.

13 Sponsorship has been received from a number of ....

Questions 14–20

Label the plan below.

Write NO MORE THAN THREE WORDS for each answer.

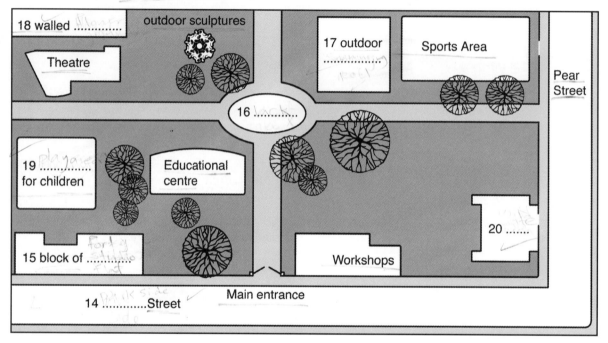

Stop the recording when you hear 'That is the end of Section 2'. Now check your answers.

Further practice for Listening Sections 1 and 2

The questions below help you make sure you have chosen the correct answers for questions 1–20 in Sections 1 and 2.

Personal details

Before you listen, use these questions to help you predict when to listen carefully for the answers.

Predict the type of questions which are asked to obtain information.

*Look at **Questions 1–4** on page 8. What questions can the Receptionist ask to obtain the information? You can use the following: What/How/How long …? or Can/Could you tell me …?*

1 ....
....

2 ....
....

3 ....
....

4 ....
....

Completing sentences

*Look at **Questions 7–10** on page 9 and answer the following:*

1   Which word or phase in each list below is **not** related to the word in italics?

7	*departure*	start (out) date you want to leave return date go away when
8	*cost*	price fee pay save how much
9	*discount*	reduction additional charge less (money) off special offer
10	*booking*	reservation part-payment reserve cancellation put name down for

2   Does the Receptionist provide all the information in questions 7–10? ....

3   Which questions or statements are likely to be used in each case below?

Question 7

.... *when*

.... *(?)*

Question 8

How ....

....?

Question 9

What ....

....?

Question 10

I'll just give ....

....

Gap-filling

It is important that you develop the skill of predicting the content of each gap to be filled.

*Look at **Questions 11–13** on page 10 and decide whether a noun, adjective verb or adverb is needed.*

11 ....

12 ....

13 ....

Understanding plans

*Look at **Questions 14–20** in Section 2.*

To help you to see the organisation of the plans, use the following words to describe where the places 14–20 in the plan of the park on page 10 are:

centre	corner	park	hand	right
left	bottom	top	entrance	side
in	on	near	beside	near
below	above			

Example:

14   is at the bottom of the plan.

15   is ....

....

16   is ....

....

17   is ....

....

18   is ....

....

19   is ....

....

20   is ....

....

Now check your answers to these exercises. When you have done so, listen again to Sections 1 and 2 of the test and decide whether you wish to change any of your answers on pages 8–10. Then check your answers to Sections 1 and 2 of the test.

Section 3   Questions 21–30

Questions 21–23

Choose the correct letter A, B or C.

21 Generally, Rosana finds the Wednesday programme

    A worthless.
    B very slow.
    C valuable.

22 Rosana wants to change her course because

    A she always arrives home very late at night.
    B it affects her work on the next two days.
    C she doesn't get on with the course tutors.

23 If Rosana changes her course, she

    A may not have the same tutor.
    B cannot change her mind again.
    C may regret the change.

Questions 24 and 25

Choose TWO letters A–E.

Which TWO good things about the distance-learning component are mentioned?

    A course length

    B evening seminars

    C course tutors

    D course flexibility

    E time factor

Questions 26–30

Complete the summary below.

Write NO MORE THAN THREE WORDS AND/OR A NUMBER for each answer.

Course Assessment

Students are required to keep a written **26** .... and present a paper monthly. Thirty per cent of the marks are allocated to the **27** .... Each student has to keep a **28** .... portfolio which in the end accounts for **29** .... of their marks. Each student is also expected to present at least one piece of work at a **30** ....

Stop the recording when you hear 'That is the end of Section 3'. Now check your answers.

Section 4   Questions 31–40

Questions 31–37

Choose the correct letter A, B, or C.

31 The purpose of the data collection was to

    A test people's reaction to different buildings.
    B collect detailed information on various buildings.
    C assess the beauty of different public buildings.

32 The initial plan to use a questionnaire was abandoned, because

    A it would take too much time to produce.
    B the questions were too difficult to write.
    C it would take too long for people to complete.

33 People indicated their reactions on a 1–5 scale,

    A giving rise to some interesting answers.
    B ensuring that the information was easier to collect.
    C making it quicker to choose the top three images.

34 To make sure people could see the detail in the images better

    A only daylight images were used.
    B black and white images were used.
    C the images were produced in colour.

35 What was done to preserve the images when being used?

    A they were covered in plastic with a special machine.
    B people were asked to wear gloves when touching them.
    C the images were handled only by the researcher.

36 Among the people who formed part of the sample were

    A tourists from various places.
    B office workers during lunch-break.
    C commuters as they exited stations.

37 What was the reason for appointing a leader for the group?

    A to comply with the instructions for the task.
    B to help hold the team together.
    C to allocate tasks to the various members.

Questions 38–40

Which findings match the age groups of the image testing?

Write the appropriate letter A–D next to each age group.

Findings
A varied reaction
B mainly scored 1
C mostly scored 3
D mainly scored 5

38 11–18 year-olds   ....

39 20–40 year-olds   ....

40 50 years old and over   ....

Stop the recording when you hear 'That is the end of Section 4'. Now check your answers.

Reading   Academic Reading 60 minutes

Reading Passage 1

*You should spend about 20 minutes on **Questions 1–13**, which are based on Reading Passage 1 on the following pages.*

Questions 1–4

Reading passage 1 has five sections **A–E.**

*Choose the correct heading for sections **B–E** from the list of headings below.*

*Write the correct number, **i–viii**, in boxes **1–4** on your answer sheet.*

List of Headings
i How the problem of land scarcity has been overcome in the past
ii Various predictions about future solutions to a lack of space
iii The effects of population growth on land availability
iv The importance of the new British Library
v An expanding population
vi A description of a mega-city
vii A firm belief that human habitation of outer space will occur
viii The importance of having an international space station

Example	Answer
Section **A**	**v**

1   Section B

2   Section C

3   Section D

4   Section E

Space

Is humanity running out of space or will we find new frontiers?

As populations grow, people have to look for more innovative ways to provide space.

Section A

The world has changed dramatically since Thomas Malthus's work *An Essay on the Principle of Population*, first published in 1798, argued that by the mid 1800s the unrestricted expansion of the human population would outgrow the agricultural land available to supply humanity with food. Over 150 years have passed since this theoretical milestone, but mankind, admittedly somewhat more cramped, is still expanding and will continue to do so.

Section B

The impact of unfettered population growth is clear for all to see. Urbanization is now a more evident worldwide phenomenon than

previously as even greater numbers of people drift from rural areas to vast cities all over the world like Tokyo, Mexico City and Mumbai (26.4 million, 18.4 million and 18.1 million inhabitants in 2000 respectively) in their quest for a better life. These mega-cities, i.e. conurbations with an estimated population of more than 10 million people, are springing up in every continent. Now teeming with humanity, they are hungry for one increasingly valuable resource: land.

While developments in agricultural technology ensure humanity may be able, by and large, to feed the people flocking to these great metropolises, the expansion of the human race is fuelling an unprecedented appetite for real estate. Space, whether it be for personal or public use, corporate or national, human or flora/fauna, is now at a premium as we move into a new century. Not only is more land required for accommodation, but also for a wide range of infrastructure facilities. Transport systems including roads within and between cities need to be constructed or upgraded to create motorways; green fields are turned into airports; virgin forest is stripped to provide food and firewood. In poorer regions, this newly exposed land becomes desert, completing the cycle of destruction.

Section C

Hitherto, the most common practice for the utilization of expensive space for living and working has been to build upwards; hence, the demand for ever higher buildings, both apartment and commercial, in major cities like New York, Shanghai and Singapore all vying with each other for the tallest buildings. There has also been a tradition for building underground, not just for transport systems, but for the storage of waste, depositories for books etc. as in London, where The British Library housing millions of books has been built largely underground.

Recent years have seen more novel construction developments around the world. In the past, in many countries, Holland and the UK included, marshes and flood plains have been reclaimed from the sea. Like the city of Venice in Italy, housing complexes and even airports have now been constructed off-shore to amazing effect. In Japan, Kansai International Airport has been built off-shore on a man-made island at vast expense and in Dubai a very imaginative and expensive housing complex in the shape of a palm tree is being built just off the coast on land created by a construction company. However, these and other developments are at risk from rising sea levels as a consequence of global warming.

Section D

But where will the human race go when planet earth is full? There have been many theories put forward about the human population moving to outer space. Marshall Savage (1992, 1994), for example, has projected that the human population will reach five quintillion throughout the solar system by the year 3000, with the majority living in the asteroid belt. Arthur C Clarke, a fervent supporter of Savage, now argues that by the year 2057 there will be humans on the Moon, Mars, Europa, Ganymede, Titan and in orbit around Venus, Neptune and Pluto. Feeman Dyson (1999) favours the Kuiper belt as the future home of humanity, suggesting this could happen within a few centuries.

Section E

Habitation in outer space in huge stations is no longer just a dream, but a reality. A permanent international space station now orbits the earth. The first commercial tourist recently went into outer space with more trips planned for the near future. This is only a beginning, but the development of space hotels is not far-off. There is no knowing where mankind may end up. But the ideas about off-world habitation are not fanciful and I am sure I am not alone in fantasizing about summer holidays spent watching the moons rising in some far-flung planet or on a floating hotel somewhere on the Andromeda nebula.

Questions 5–8

Complete the sentences below.

*Choose **NO MORE THAN TWO WORDS** from the passage for each answer.*

Write your answers in boxes 5–8 on your answer sheet.

5   The movement of rural people to cities is a ....

6   Land is now a very .... , as a result of the growing demand for space.

7   The feeding of the human race will perhaps be guaranteed by changes in ....

8   Besides the demands of accommodation, land is needed for various ....

Questions 9–13

Do the following statements agree with the claims of the writer in Reading Passage 1?

In boxes 9–13 on your answer sheet write

YES   *if the statement reflects the claims of the writer*
NO   *if the statement contradicts the claims of the writer*
NOT GIVEN   *if it is impossible to say what the writer thinks about this*

9   The destruction of land for food and firewood is linked to desertification.

10   Shortage of space has also led to underground building construction.

11   The building of the airport in Japan cost much more than that of the housing complex in Dubai.

12   Arthur C Clarke was the only person to predict that mankind will inhabit other parts of the solar system.

13   The concept of the habitation of outer space by mankind is unimaginable.

Before you check your answers to Reading Passage 1, go on to pages 19–20.

Further practice for Reading Passage 1

The questions below help you make sure that you have chosen the correct answers for questions 1–4 in Reading Passage 1.

Title

Look at the title of the passage and answer the following questions.

1 Does the title give you information about a problem?

....

2 Can you predict the contents of the article?

....

3 Does the title contain a cause and effect?

....

Section A and example

Look at Section A and the example answer. Answer these questions.

1 Do you think it is important to look at the example?

....

2 Does the introduction describe a problem?

....

3 Is the word *cramped* at the end of the paragraph positive?

....

4 In the rest of the article, do you expect to see effects and solutions?

....

Question 1

Look at Section B and answer these questions.

1 Does section B describe the effects of section A?

....

2 Does the section contain words related to effect?

....

3 Does the first paragraph relate to effects and the second to solutions?

....

Question 2

Look at Section C and answer these questions.

1 Does the section talk about the future? Look at the tenses, adverbs of time and nouns.

....

2 Does the section contain causes?

....

3 Does the section contain different ways used to solve the problem of the lack of space?

....

Question 3

Look at Section D and answer these questions.

1   Does the section talk about the future? Look at the tenses and time phrases.

....

2   Is the time clear without reading the paragraph in detail?

....

3   Is the section about predictions?

....

Question 4

Look at Section E and answer these questions.

1   Is the section only about the space station?

....

2   Are there words and phrases connected with certainty?

....

3   Does the section tell you what the writer believes?

....

4   Read the titles for sections A to E. Do they fit together?

....

Now check your answers to these exercises. When you have done so, decide whether you wish to change any of your answers to Reading Passage 1 on pages 15 and 18. Then check your answers to Reading Passage 1.

Reading Passage 2

*You should spend about 20 minutes on **Questions 14–27**, which are based on Reading Passage 2 below.*

The history of salt

1   Salt is so simple and plentiful that we almost take it for granted. In chemical terms, salt is the combination of a sodium ion with a chloride ion, making it one of the most basic molecules on earth. It is also one of the most plentiful: it has been estimated that salt deposits under the state of Kansas alone could supply the entire world's needs for the next 250,000 years.

2   But salt is also an essential element. Without it, life itself would be impossible since the human body requires the mineral in order to function properly. The concentration of sodium ions in the blood is directly related to the regulation of safe body fluid levels. And while we are all familiar with its many uses in cooking, we may not be aware that this element is used in some 14,000 commercial applications. From manufacturing pulp and paper to setting dyes in textiles and fabric, from producing soaps and detergents to making our roads safe in winter, salt plays an essential part in our daily lives.

3   Salt has a long and influential role in world history. From the dawn of civilization, it has been a key factor in economic, religious, social and political development. In every corner of the world, it has been the subject of superstition, folklore, and warfare, and has even been used as currency.

4   As a precious and portable commodity, salt has long been a cornerstone of economies throughout history. In fact, researcher M.R. Bloch conjectured that civilization began along the edges of the desert because of the natural surface deposits of salt found there. Bloch also believed that the first war – likely fought near the ancient city of Essalt on the Jordan River – could have been fought over the city's precious supplies of the mineral.

5   In 2200 BC, the Chinese emperor Hsia Yu levied one of the first known taxes. He taxed salt. In Tibet, Marco Polo noted that tiny cakes of salt were pressed with images of the Grand Khan to be used as coins and to this day among the nomads of Ethiopia's Danakil Plains it is still used as money. Greek slave traders often bartered it for slaves, giving rise to the expression that someone was "not worth his salt." Roman

legionnaires were paid in salt – a salarium, the Latin origin of the word "salary."

6 Merchants in 12th-century Timbuktu – the gateway to the Sahara Desert and the seat of scholars – valued this mineral as highly as books and gold. In France, Charles of Anjou levied the "gabelle," a salt tax, in 1259 to finance his conquest of the Kingdom of Naples. Outrage over the gabelle fueled the French Revolution. Though the revolutionaries eliminated the tax shortly after Louis XVI, the Republic of France re-established the gabelle in the early 19th Century; only in 1946 was it removed from the books.

7 The Erie Canal, an engineering marvel that connected the Great Lakes to New York's Hudson River in 1825, was called "the ditch that salt built." Salt tax revenues paid for half the cost of construction of the canal. The British monarchy supported itself with high salt taxes, leading to a bustling black market for the white crystal. In 1785, the earl of Dundonald wrote that every year in England, 10,000 people were arrested for salt smuggling. And protesting against British rule in 1930, Mahatma Gandhi led a 200-mile march to the Arabian Ocean to collect untaxed salt for India's poor.

8 In religion and culture, salt long held an important place with Greek worshippers consecrating it in their rituals. Further, in Buddhist tradition, salt repels evil spirits, which is why it is customary to throw it over your shoulder before entering your house after a funeral: it scares off any evil spirits that may be clinging to your back. Shinto religion also uses it to purify an area. Before sumo wrestlers enter the ring for a match – which is in reality an elaborate Shinto rite – a handful is thrown into the center to drive off malevolent spirits.

9 In the Southwest of the United States, the Pueblo worship the Salt Mother. Other native tribes had significant restrictions on who was permitted to eat salt. Hopi legend holds that the angry Warrior Twins punished mankind by placing valuable salt deposits far from civilization, requiring hard work and bravery to harvest the precious mineral. In 1933, the Dalai Lama was buried sitting up in a bed of salt. Today, a gift of salt endures in India as a potent symbol of good luck and a reference to Mahatma Gandhi's liberation of India.

10 The effects of salt deficiency are highlighted in times of war, when human bodies and national economies are strained to their limits. Thousands of Napoleon's troops died during the French retreat from Moscow due to inadequate wound healing and lowered resistance to disease – the results of salt deficiency.

Questions 14–16

*Choose **THREE** letters A–H.*

*Write your answers in boxes **14–16** on your answer sheet.*

NB Your answers may be given in any order.

*Which **THREE** statements are true of salt?*

    A   A number of cities take their name from the word *salt*.

    B   Salt contributed to the French Revolution.

    C   The uses of salt are countless.

    D   Salt has been produced in China for less than 2000 years.

    E   There are many commercial applications for salt.

    F   Salt deposits in the state of Kansas are vast.

    G   Salt has few industrial uses nowadays.

    H   Slaves used salt as a currency.

Questions 17–21

Complete the summary.

*Choose **NO MORE THAN TWO WORDS** from the passage for each answer.*

*Write your answers in boxes **17–21** on your answer sheet.*

Salt is such an **17** .... that people would not be able to live without it. As well as its uses in cooking, this basic mineral has thousands of business **18** .... ranging from making paper to the manufacture of soap. Being a prized and **19** .... , it has played a major part in the economies of many countries. As such, salt has not only led to war, but has also been used to raise **20** .... by governments in many parts of the world. There are also many instances of its place in religion and culture, being used as a means to get rid of evil **21** ....

Questions 22–27

Do the following statements agree with the information in Reading Passage 2?

In boxes 22–27 on your answer sheet write

TRUE   *if the statement agrees with the information*
FALSE   *if the statement contradicts the information*
NOT GIVEN   *if there is no information about the statement*

22 It has been suggested that salt was responsible for the first war.

23 The first tax on salt was imposed by a Chinese emperor.

24 Salt is no longer used as a form of currency.

25 Most of the money for the construction of the Erie Canal came from salt taxes.

26 Hopi legend believes that salt deposits were placed far away from civilization to penalize mankind.

27 A lack of salt is connected with the deaths of many of Napoleon's soldiers during the French retreat from Moscow.

Before you check your answers to Reading Passage 2, go on to pages 25–26.

Further practice for Reading Passage 2

The questions below help you make sure that you have chosen the correct answers for questions 22–27 in Reading Passage 2.

Question 22

Look at the fourth paragraph and answer these questions.

1   Did Bloch know for certain what caused the first war?

   ....

2   Do the words *It has been suggested* in the question mean that the information is not certain?

   ....

3   Does the question suggest that salt was the cause?

   ....

4   In the passage, do the words *fought over* show a connection (cause and effect) between salt and war?

   ....

Question 23

Look at the fifth paragraph and answer these questions.

1   Does the reading passage say the tax was one of the first known taxes?

   ....

2   Do you know whether it was the first tax on salt?

   ....

3   Is it possible that a salt tax was introduced elsewhere but not known about?

   ....

Question 24

Look at the fifth paragraph and answer these questions.

1   Are the words *no longer* in the question important?

   ....

2   Does a phrase like *to this day/still* contradict the words *no longer*?

   ....

3   If you remove the phrase *no longer*, does it change the answer?

   ....

4   Is the past tense used at the end of the third sentence in the reading passage?

   ....

Question 25

Look at the seventh paragraph and answer these questions.

1   Does the name *Erie* help you find the information?

   ....

2   Does the word *most* refer to a quantity?

   ....

3   Is a quantity given in the passage?

   ....

4   If so, is the quantity in the question the same as the quantity in the passage?

   ....

Question 26

Look at the ninth paragraph and answer these questions.

1   Does the name *Hopi* help you find the information easily?

    ....

2   Are the words *penalize* and *punishment* related?

    ....

3   Does the paragraph give a reason why salt was placed far away?

    ....

Question 27

Look at the last paragraph and answer these questions.

1   Are there any words in the paragraph which show a relationship between salt and death?

    ....

2   Is the relationship cause and effect?

    ....

Now check your answers to these exercises. When you have done so, decide whether you wish to change any of your answers to Reading Passage 2. Then check your answers to Reading Passage 2.

Reading Passage 3

*You should spend about 20 minutes on **Questions 28–40**, which are based on Reading Passage 3 below.*

Volunteering:
enriching others and helping oneself

A Volunteering, some might mistakenly think, embraces a plethora of people from all walks of life as well as activities, but data from the other side of the world suggest otherwise. A 2001 survey on who participated in volunteering by the Office for National Statistics (ONS) in the United Kingdom (UK) revealed that people in higher income households are more likely than others to volunteer. In England and Wales, 57 per cent of adults with gross annual household incomes of £75,000 or more, have volunteered formally (such as raising or handling money for a charity or being a member of a committee) in the 12 months prior to the survey date. They were almost twice as likely to have done so than those living in households with an annual income under £10,000.

B As well as having high household incomes, volunteers also tend to have higher academic qualifications, be in higher socio-economic groups and be in employment. Among people with a degree or postgraduate qualification, 79 per cent had volunteered informally and 57 per cent had volunteered formally in the previous 12 months. For people with no qualifications the corresponding proportions were 52 per cent and 23 per cent. But voluntary work is certainly not the exclusive preserve of the rich, nor should it be. Does the answer not lie perhaps in the fact that the rich tend to have money to allow them the time to become involved in voluntary work compared to less well-off people?

C A breakdown in the year 2000 of the range of volunteering activities taken from The Australian Bureau of Statistics gives an idea of the scale of activities in which people are typically involved. Eleven sectors are given ranging from Community and Welfare, which accounted for just over a quarter of the total hours volunteered in Australia, to Law/justice/politics with 1.2 percent at the other end of the scale. Other fields included sport/recreation, religious activities and education, following at 21.2 per cent, 16.9 and 14.3 per cent respectively. Foreign/international volunteer work accounted for 2.4 per cent of the total hours. The data here also seem to point to a cohort of volunteers with expertise and experience.

D The knock-on effect of volunteering on the lives of individuals can be profound. Voluntary work helps foster independence and imparts the ability to deal with different situations, often simultaneously, thus teaching people how to work their way through different systems. It therefore brings people into touch with the real world; and, hence, equips them for the future.

E Initially, young adults in their late teens might not seem to have the expertise or knowledge to impart to others that say a teacher or agriculturalist or nurse would have, but they do have many skills that can help others. And in the absence of any particular talent, their energy and enthusiasm can be harnessed for the benefit of their fellow human beings, and ultimately themselves. From all this, the gain to any community no matter how many volunteers are involved is immeasurable.

F Employers will generally look favourably on people who have shown an ability to work as part of a team. It demonstrates a willingness to learn and an independent spirit, which would be desirable qualities in any employee. So to satisfy employers' demands for experience when applying for work, volunteering can act as a means of gaining experience that might otherwise elude would-be workers and can ultimately lead to paid employment in the desired field.

G But what are the prerequisites for becoming a volunteer? One might immediately think of attributes like kindness, selflessness, strength of character, ability to deal with others, determination, adaptability and flexibility and a capacity to comprehend the ways of other people. While offering oneself selflessly, working as a volunteer makes further demands on the individual. It requires a strength of will, a sense of moral responsibility for one's fellow

human beings, and an ability to fit into the ethos of an organization or community. But it also requires something which in no way detracts from the valuable work done by volunteers and which may seem at first glance both contradictory and surprising: self-interest.

H Organizations involved in any voluntary work have to be realistic about this. If someone, whatever the age, is going to volunteer and devote their time without money, they do need to receive something from it for themselves. People who are unemployed can use volunteer work as a stepping-stone to employment or as a means of finding out whether they really like the field they plan to enter or as a way to help them find themselves.

I It is tempting to use some form of community work as an alternative to national service or as punishment for petty criminals by making the latter for example clean up parks, wash away graffiti, work with victims of their own or of other people. This may be acceptable, but it does not constitute volunteer work, two cardinal rules of which are the willingness to volunteer without coercion and working unpaid.

Questions 28–33

Reading Passage 3 has nine paragraphs **A–I**.

Which paragraph contains the following information?

*Write the correct letter, **A–I**, in boxes **28–33** on your answer sheet.*

28 a description of what does not satisfy the criteria for volunteer work

29 the impact of voluntary work on the development of individuals

30 the requirement for both selflessness and self-interest in volunteers

31 various areas in which people volunteer

32 the benefit of voluntary work for the young

33 a mistaken view of volunteering

Questions 34–37

Choose the correct letters A, B, C or D.

Write the correct letter in boxes 34–37 on your answer sheet.

34 The ONS survey was done to find out

    A why people undertook volunteering.
    B how many people participated in volunteering.
    C how many rich people did volunteer work.
    D which people were involved in volunteering.

35 The ONS survey found that people with university qualifications were

    A as likely to volunteer as those with no qualifications.
    B more likely to volunteer than those with no qualifications.
    C less likely to volunteer than those with no qualifications.
    D the only group likely to do formal volunteer work.

36 It is suggested that rich people volunteer as a result of having

    A clearer goals.
    B fewer children.
    C more spare time.
    D greater guilt.

37 Volunteer work benefits people by teaching them how to

    A function in systems.
    B communicate clearly.
    C deal with failure.
    D overcome shyness.

Questions 38–40

Complete each sentence with the correct ending, A–F below.

Write the correct letter, A–F, in boxes 38–40 on your answer sheet.

38 One of the requirements of being a volunteer is being able to

39 Volunteering can be used as a way for the unemployed to

40 Employers in general tend to

A	consider workers with volunteer work experience an asset.
B	gain a very well paid job.
C	gain access to a job in a field of interest.
D	benefit most from volunteer work.
E	understand how people behave.
F	want much younger workers.

Writing    Academic Writing 60 minutes

WRITING TASK 1

You should spend about 20 minutes on this task.

The graph below shows the number of passenger railway journeys made in Great Britain between 1950 and 2004/5.

Summarize the information by selecting and reporting the main features, and make comparisons where relevant.

Write at least 150 words.

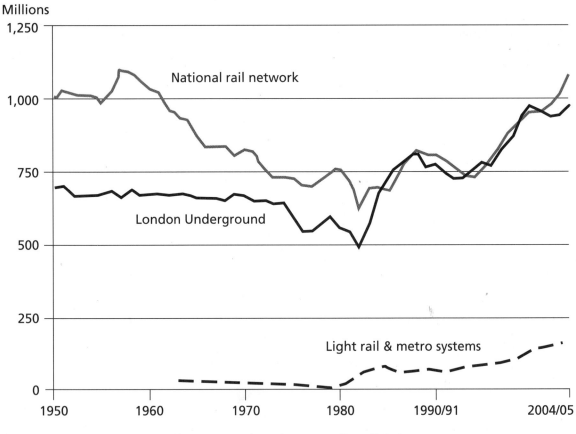

Passenger railway journeys, Great Britain

Before you write your answer to Task 1, go on to pages 31–33.

Further practice for Writing Task 1

Language to describe movements in graphs

1 *Look at the list of verbs opposite and match them to the parts of the graphs A–I.*

to plunge ....

to soar ....

to rise (gradually) ....

to fluctuate ....

to hit/reach a peak ....

to dip ....

to bottom out ....

to remain flat ....

> **Example**
>
> to fall ....A...........

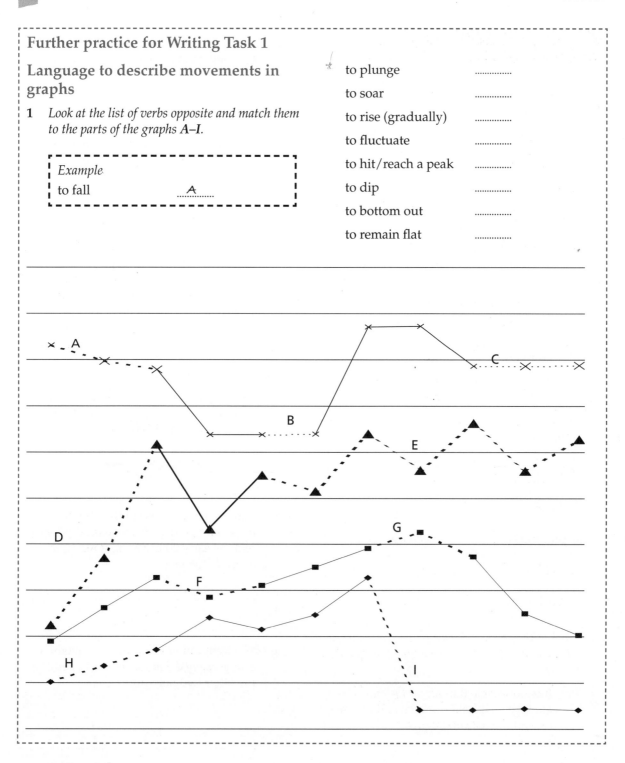

2   *Complete the following sentences using words from 1 above as either verbs or nouns in the correct form.*

   a   Student numbers .... wildly, but the trend was clearly upward.

   b   There was a gradual .... in student numbers, followed by a sharp drop.

   c   Student numbers .... a peak towards the end of the period and then declined steadily.

   d   There was a steady .... in student numbers, after which they fell and then bottomed out.

   e   The number of students ...., but then they began to climb again.

   f   After plunging sharply, student numbers .... out.

   g   After an initial rise, student numbers .... to a new low.

3   *Match the following verbs with the correct verb from 1 above.*

   Example   go down = fall, dip

decline	....	rocket	....
plummet	....	decrease	....
increase	....	jump	....
reach a high	....	level off	....

4   *Look at the graph in **Task 1** on page 30. Correct the sentences below by rearranging the words in italics.*

   a   It is noticeable that *the for the numbers Underground London* match and at times exceed the national figures.

   ....

   ....

   b   Generally speaking, all three networks *trend an upward show.*

   ....

   ....

   c   By 2004/05, the National rail network *a high had reached of billion around 1.1* passenger journeys.

   ....

   ....

   d   Moreover, journey numbers for the London Underground showed a similar pattern *500 from falling about approximately 700 million to* million.

   ....

   ....

   e   The graph illustrates passenger journeys on *systems three in Great railway Britain* between 1950 and 2005.

   ....

   ....

   f   Both systems exceeded the billion passenger journey mark, with the 1980s and the early 2000s *the most increases noticeable witnessing.*

   ....

   ....

   g   The light railway and metro systems *have as many did not as passenger journeys* the other two networks.

   ....

   ....

   h   The most striking characteristic is that the journey numbers for the National rail network *Underground the correspond to those for London.*

   ....

   ....

5   *Decide which sentences **a–h** in **4** above are:*

   i   summarizing sentences

   ii   comparisons

   iii an introduction

   iv   striking features

   Note that some sentences may be included in more than one category.

6   *Now write your own answer to **Task 1** on page 30. When you have finished writing, use questions **a–g** below to check your answer.*

   a   Is the text at least 150 words?

   ....

   b   Is the text divided into paragraphs?

   ....

   c   Does the introduction contain words and phrases that are different from the question?

   ....

   d   Has the text summarized the information by selecting and reporting the main features and made relevant comparisons?

   ....

   e   Is anything missing?

   ....

   f   Does the text avoid repetition of words and grammar?

   ....

   g   Are there any mistakes?

   ....

7   *Now look at the following model answer for **Task 1** and answer questions **6 a–g** again.*

> The graph provides information about how many trips were made by passengers on three railway systems in *Great Britain* between 1950 and 2004/5.
>
> It is clear that the trends for all three networks are upward with the most striking feature being the similarity between the National rail network and the London Underground. For example, numbers for the former fell from approximately one billion passengers in 1950 to about 750 million in the early 1980s. Likewise, the London Underground experienced a parallel, but less pronounced, decline over the same period (from approximately 700 million to about 500 million). Thereafter, both followed a very similar pattern as they climbed towards the billion passenger mark, with the 1980s and the early 2000s seeing the sharpest increases. The National rail network reached a high of approximately 1.1 billion passenger journeys in 2004/05.
>
> By comparison, after their introduction in the 1960s, the light railway and metro systems carried fewer passengers than the other two networks, no more than around ten million over the first 15 years. However, in 1980 the number of journeys made by passengers picked up, reaching nearly 200 million in 2004/05.
>
> (Word count: 188 words)

Now check your answers to this section and compare your Task 1 answer with the model above and authentic student answer on page 127. Then do Task 2 on page 34.

WRITING TASK 2

You should spend about 40 minutes on this task.

Write about the following topic:

> *The inequality between rich and poor nations is now wider than it has ever been before.*
> *What do you think are the main causes of this difference and what do you think can be done*
> *to reduce the gap?*

Give reasons for your answer and include any relevant examples from your own
knowledge or experience.

Write at least 250 words.

Speaking 11–14 minutes

PART 1   Introduction (4–5 minutes)

The examiner will ask you about yourself, and topics which are familiar to you.

EXAMPLE

Places in your hometown
- Can you tell me your name?
- Where do you come from?
- Describe the place where you were born.
- Tell me about the main types of buildings there.
- How easy is it to get to?
- How have the buildings in your hometown changed since you were a child?

Now look at the Further Practice section on page 36.

PART 2   Individual long turn (3–4 minutes)

Describe your favourite possession.

You should say:

what this is
when you obtained it
what you like about it

and explain why this item is important for you.

You will have to talk about this topic for one to two minutes. You have one minute to think about what you are going to say. You can make some notes to help you if you wish.

Now look at the Further Practice section on page 36.

PART 3   Two-way discussion (4–5 minutes)

In this part of the exam, the examiner will discuss a topic with you. The topic is usually related in some way to the topic in Part 2, but the questions will be of a more abstract nature.

The main products that are made in your country

Example questions:

What kinds of products are manufactured in your home country?
How important are they for the local or national economy?
Is manufacturing more important in your home country now than it was in the past? In what way?

Commercialism in your country

Example questions:

What are the advantages of manufacturing consumer goods in your own country?
Have we become too obsessed nowadays with owning the latest products? Why? Why not?
What do you think are the effects of commercialism on people?

Further practice for Speaking

PART 1

After you give your details, the examiner will ask about other personal details, things you like and are familiar with.

1   *Below are some notes made by a student from China when the examiner asked the questions opposite. Match the notes a–e with the questions.*

   a   Compared to the past, they are now ... / In the past, they were ...

   b   ... easy to get there, because ...

   c   ... and made of glass and so ...

   d   .... modern and lively, as ...

   e   (Shanghai, China)

2   *What questions would you ask for the following:* **travelling** *and* **flowers**?

   ....

   ....

3   *What adjectives would you use to describe* **holidays** *and* **walking**? *Think of at least two adjectives.*

   ....

Now with a partner, practise asking and answering the questions on the topics above.

PART 2

In the exam you have one minute to make notes about the subject on the card. Pen and paper are provided. Use this time to write very short notes to guide you.

1   *Make short notes for two or more items below. Use the example for a possession to help you.*

		possession	book	musical device	game
a	What?	iphone			
b	Description:	compact			
c	When?	week ago			
d	How?	gift			
e	Why?	convenient not live without			

2   *To organize your answer, match the phrases below to a–e in the table.*

   1   What I like most about it is ...

   2   I have chosen it because ...

   3   It's also ... and so ...

   4   It reminds me of ...

   5   If I didn't have it ...

   6   I would like to choose/ talk about ...

   7   I received it last year for my birthday

   8   My favourite ...

   9   It's got a ...

   10   I like it because it's ...

3   *Now make notes for the other items in the table. Use your notes to talk on one or more subjects for one to two minutes.*

TEST TWO

Section 1   Questions 1–10

Questions 1–10

Complete the notes below.

*Write **NO MORE THAN THREE WORDS AND/OR A NUMBER** for each answer.*

Sidney Street Community Centre

Venue booking form

> *Example*   *Answer*
> Name   ..Maria.. Lincoln

Details of party booking

Number of people	**1** approximately ....
Date of party	**2** ....
Name of room	The **3** ....
Time	**4** from .... to .... pm
Drinks	Licensed only for soft drinks

Contact details

Postcode	**5** ....
Address	Flat **6** ...., 35 Beeches Street

Telephone:

Landline	22 32 79
Mobile	07897 **7** ....

Booking fee

Cost of room hire	£115 with **8** ....
Disco system hire	Optional. Fee £25 with no technician.
Deposit	**9** £...............
Insurance	£9 for 24 hours. Covers cancellation, **10** ....

Stop the recording when you hear 'That is the end of Section 1.' Now check your answers.

Section 2   Questions 11–20

Questions 11–13

Choose the correct letter A, B or C.

11 Green products are aimed at

    A people who can afford to pay the higher prices.
    B the young who are very environmentally aware.
    C those who care more about the environment.

12 Grass roofs have been used

    A on buildings in Europe.
    B on homes and other buildings.
    C mostly on residential buildings.

13 On the grass roof, soil or crushed stones are laid directly on top of

    A the insulation and drainage layer.
    B the waterproof underlay.
    C the wooden roof deck.

Questions 14–18

Complete the notes below.

*Write **ONE WORD ONLY** for each answer.*

Type of roof	Advantages	Disadvantages	Verdict
Grass roof	Cooler in summer, warmer in winter 14 Little .... Encourages biodiversity Absorbs water run-off	15 .... appearance in winter	Highly recommended
Tiles	16 .... appearance	17 .... absorption	Not recommended
Thatched roof	Good insulators	18 Very	Not ideal for cities

Questions 19 and 20

Choose **TWO** *letters A–E.*

Which **TWO** *methods for encouraging people to install grass roofs are mentioned?*

    A educating school children

    B holding design competitions

    C support from celebrities

    D making grass roofs cheaper

    E using the media

Stop the recording when you hear 'That is the end of Section 2.' Now check your answers.

Section 3   Questions 21–30

Questions 21–23

Complete the sentences below.

Write **NO MORE THAN THREE WORDS** *for each answer.*

21 Karen is planning to use an .... for her presentation.

22 Karen is also going to prepare a power-point presentation as a ....

23 Karen wants a few websites to obtain more ....

Questions 24–28

What recommendations does Dr Owen make about the websites?

Choose your answers from the box and write the letters A–G next to questions **24–28.**

A	must read
B	read recent articles
C	look at abstracts quickly
D	check links
E	scan references
F	useful
G	limited use

Example	Answer
www.kmul.org	....A....

24 investment_IT.com   ....

25 knowledge_journal.com   ....

26 IT_knowledge_review.com   ....

27 IT_online.com   ....

28 NationalStatistics.com   ....

Questions 29 and 30

Choose **TWO** *letters A–E.*

Which **TWO** *things should be avoided in the presentation?*

   A too much information at once

   B irrelevant visuals

   C small font

   D too many colours

   E talking fast

Stop the recording when you hear 'That is the end of Section 3'.
Before you check your answers to Section 3 of the test, go on to page 41.

Further practice for Listening Section 3

In this Section, you will hear two or three people talking with each other about an academic subject.

Recommendations

Questions 24–28

Look at A–G on page 40 and answer the following questions:

Look at **A**: Does this mean that the website is essential to look at?

....

Look at **B**: Could *recent* mean over the last university term?

....

Look at **C**: Does this mean to skim to get a general idea?

....

Look at **D**: Does *check* mean look at everything in detail?

....

Look at **E**: Do *references* mean the authors of the articles?

....

Look at **F**: If something is *beneficial*, is it useful?

....

Look at **G**: Does *limited* mean that there are lots of things that are useful?

....

Things to avoid

Questions 29 and 30

Look at A–E in Questions 29 and 30 and match them to the reasons 1–5 below.

1   because people won't understand what the pictures mean and won't listen

2   because people will find it hard to keep up with you

3   because people will not be able to take in lots of details on the screen

4   because people will have difficulty reading small letters

5   because people will be puzzled about the meaning of the colours

Now check your answers to these exercises. When you have done so, listen again to Section 3 of the test and decide whether you wish to change any of your answers. Then check your answers to Section 3 of the test.

Section 4   Questions 31–40

Questions 31–40

Complete the notes below.

Write **NO MORE THAN THREE WORDS AND/OR A NUMBER** *for each answer.*

Department of the Printed Word

Statistics

- many different full- and part-time courses
- 17 students on the **31** .... MA course and 7 full-time research students
- 9 full-time lecturers
- about **32** .... per cent of students are from outside the country

Sponsorship

- links with organizations in the publishing world
- sponsorship of students, technicians and **33** ....
- outside speakers
- workshops built to expand facilities for book binding and **34** ....

Teaching

- main work is teaching the **35** ....
- as most printing is now very technological, students have to be **36** ....
- for students without the necessary skills, there are specialist technicians who deliver **37** .... in computing

Facilities

- in printing, editing, page design and layout, book-binding
- former students are now working as expert book **38** .... and ....nists

Research

- growing interest in the history of the printed word from early European etc printing techniques
- a visiting lecturer, Dr Yu, is an expert on early Chinese manuscripts and **39** .... machine
- department is very popular, with many **40** .... for each research position

---

Stop the recording when you hear 'That is the end of Section 4'.
Before you check your answers to Section 4 of the test, go on to page 43.

Further practice for Listening Section 4

In Section 4 you often need to read a lot of information as well as listen. There is usually no break in the middle (as in the other sections) to give you time to read. Skim the questions to get a summary of the listening. Read the sub-headings. Listen to the introduction to the Section.

Key words

Look at **questions 31–40** *and write which words will help you predict when to listen carefully for the answers.*

31 ....

32 ....

33 ....

34 ....

35 ....

36 ....

37 ....

38 ....

39 ....

40 ....

Grammar

Decide whether the answer in **questions 31–40** *is a number, noun, adjective, verb or adverb and circle the correct answer. Decide whether the nouns are singular or plural.*

31 number   noun   adjective   verb   adverb

....

32 number   noun   adjective   verb   adverb

....

33 number   noun   adjective   verb   adverb

....

34 number   noun   adjective   verb   adverb

....

35 number   noun   adjective   verb   adverb

....

36 number   noun   adjective   verb   adverb

....

37 number   noun   adjective   verb   adverb

....

38 number   noun   adjective   verb   adverb

....

39 number   noun   adjective   verb   adverb

....

40 number   noun   adjective   verb   adverb

....

Questions about the questions

31 Do MA courses always involve just research?

....

32 Is this a percentage?

....

33 Is this list to do with types of books?

....

34 Is this linked to doing something to books?

....

35 Is this to do with an aspect of printing?

....

36 Is this to do with being able to use computers?

....

37 Is this connected with 36?

....

38 Is this to do with fixing books?

....

39 Is this to do with the title at the top of the page?

....

40 Is this to do with something people make to a university?

....

Now check your answers to these exercises. When you have done so, listen again to Section 4 of the test and decide whether you wish to change any of your answers. Then check your answers to Section 4 of the test.

Reading

Academic Reading 60 minutes

Reading Passage 1

*You should spend about 20 minutes on **Questions 1–13**, which are based on Reading Passage 1 below.*

Seaweed for human consumption

Seaweeds are algae that live in the sea or in brackish water. Scientists often call them 'benthic marine algae', which just means 'attached algae that live in the sea'. Seaweeds come in three basic colours: red, green, and brown: dulse is the red seaweed; sea lettuce is amongst the green algae; and the brown is a wrack. Red and brown algae are almost exclusively marine, whilst green algae are also common in freshwater and in terrestrial situations. Many of these algae are very ancient organisms, and although lumped together as 'algae' are not actually closely related, having representatives in four of the five kingdoms of organisms. There are about 10,500 species of seaweeds, of which 6,500 are red algae (Rhodophyta).

The trend today is to refer to marine algae used as food as 'sea-vegetables'. The main species used in Ireland at present are dulse, carrageen moss, and various kelps and wracks. Dulse – also known as dillisk in a number of areas – is a red alga that is eaten

on both sides of the North Atlantic. Generally only eaten in Ireland after it has been dried, it is frequently sold in small packets, most commonly in the west and north. About 16 tonnes are used in Ireland at present; the species is also eaten in Canada, Iceland, Norway, France and Scotland. About 53 tonnes of carrageen moss were gathered in Ireland in 1994.

Whilst dulse and carrageen moss are worthy sea-vegetables with a history of utilisation and a small but proven market, other species also show considerable promise. Our kelp resources are considerably under-utilised. All of the kelp species are edible but *Laminaria saccharina* is probably the most palatable as it has a somewhat sweet taste, probably due to its high levels of mannitol, and it also cooks better.

Two other brown algae with potential as food are currently under investigation by us: *Himanthalia elongata*, known in some places as thongweed, and *Alaria esculenta*, also known as dabberlocks or murlins. *Himanthalia* is eaten in France after drying or pickling ('Spaghettis de mer'), and plants are sold in Ireland dried. After soaking in water it makes a surprisingly fine accompaniment to a mixed salad; it does not have the strong seaweedy taste that some dislike. With the aid of a basic research grant from Forbairt, the Irish research and development body, we are examining the growth and life cycle of populations of this species on the west coast. Plants are easy to collect but must be dried quickly and packaged well to preserve their excellent taste and mouth feel.

Alaria is a large, kelp-like brown alga that grows on exposed shores. In Ireland, plants grow to considerable sizes, being found up to 6m in length in some areas, but these are dwarfed by some Pacific species that may grow to 18m in length and to 2m in width. With Marine Research Measure funding, a study of the possibility of developing fast-growing hybrids of this species by crossing species from the Atlantic and Pacific is being carried out. We have growing in culture isolates of *A. esculenta* from Ireland, Scotland, France, Norway, and Atlantic Canada and other species from British Columbia and Japan. Species of this genus are ideal for cross-breeding studies as the males and females are tiny filamentous plants that are relatively easy to grow and propagate in culture under red light which stimulates reproduction in our growth rooms. Male and female reproductive structures occur on different plants so that we can put plants from one country in with those from another to see if they are sexually compatible.

To date, we have obtained interesting results with *A. praelonga*, a large species from Japan that co-operates sexually with *A. esculenta* from the Aran Islands and other Irish sites. The resulting Irish/Japanese progeny are grown initially in sample bottles agitated on a small shaker and their growth rates compared with plants that have resulted from self crosses. Preliminary results are very encouraging, with hybrid plants showing relatively high growth rates. We hope by this method to obtain sterile hybrids that will not reproduce in the wild so that we can introduce foreign genetic material without the fear that some sort of a tryffid will be introduced that will take over the west coast of Ireland.

While studies of these two food species are very promising, we must bear in mind that the market for such sea-vegetables is very small and needs development and investment. Nutritionally, sea-vegetables are as good as any land-vegetable and are superior in their vitamin, trace element and even protein content. The increase in catholic food tastes in Europe should see greater utilisation of sea-vegetables in the next 20 years.

Questions 1–5

Classify the following features as characterizing

A brown algae

B green algae

C red algae

D brown and red algae

Write the correct letter A, B, C or D in boxes 1–5 on your answer sheet.

1   are being investigated as possible food sources.

2   are now called sea-vegetables.

3   make up more than half of all seaweed species.

4   are found on land and in freshwater.

5   are nearly all marine.

Questions 6–9

Complete the table below.

Choose NO MORE THAN THREE WORDS from Reading Passage 1 for each answer.

Write your answers in boxes 6–9 on your answer sheet.

Types of brown algae	Himanthalia elongata	Alaria esculenta
Potential	food	food
Common name	thongweed	dabberlocks or 6 ....
Research funded	with a 7 .... from Forbairt	by Marine Research Measure
Purpose	to examine growth and life cycle populations	creation of fast-growing 8 ....
Advantage	easy to collect	just right for 9 ....

Questions 10–13

Answer the questions below.

Choose NO MORE THAN THREE WORDS from the passage for each answer.

Write your answers in boxes 10–13 on your answer sheet.

10   What does the red light in the growth rooms do?

11   What are initial growth rates shown to be?

12   What does the sea-vegetable market need?

13   What increasingly should lead to greater consumption of sea-vegetables?

Before you check your answers to Reading Passage 1, go on to page 47.

Further practice for Reading Passage 1

The questions below will help you make sure that you have chosen the correct answers for questions 1–5 in Reading Passage 1.

Classification

To classify features, you need to match information.

*Look at the categories **A–D** and Questions **1–5** and answer the following.*

1   Is it better to find the colour categories first and put a box around each one?

....

2   Do you need to go beyond paragraphs 1–3 and the first line of paragraph 4?

....

3   Are the colour categories in the same order in the passage and the questions?

....

4   Which words from each feature 1–5 can you use to scan between the boxes?

   1 ....   2 ....   3 ....

   4 ....   5 ....

5   Do you need to read the passage in detail as you scan for these words?

....

6   Do any of the words in 1–5 relate to quantity / numbers?

....

7   Is it necessary to match all of the features in order?

....

8   Does the name *green algae* show a connection with land plants?

....

9   Does *almost exclusively* in the fourth sentence mean *nearly all*?

....

10 Is it easy to see the term *sea-vegetables*?

....

Now check your answers to these exercises. When you have done so, decide whether you wish to change any of your answers to Reading Passage 1. Then check your answers to Reading Passage 1.

Reading Passage 2

You should spend about 20 minutes on **Questions 14–27***, which are based on Reading Passage 2 below.*

Designing and shipping after the Restriction of Hazardous Substances (RoHS) directive

1 Almost two months after the European Union's ban on the use of six environmentally unfriendly materials went into effect, designers have clear evidence that failure to meet the Restriction of Hazardous Substances (RoHS) directive means lost sales. Palm Inc. recently announced that its Treo 650 smart phone is no longer being shipped to Europe, since it doesn't meet RoHS requirements. And several Apple Computer Inc. products will not be sold in Europe for the same reason.

2 The EU directive, which took effect on 1st July, covers lead, mercury, cadmium, hexavalent chromium, polybrominated biphenyls and polybrominated diphenyl ethers. Electronics vendors worldwide are working to eliminate those substances from nearly all new products developed for the European market, while also adapting their manufacturing processes to a lead (Pb)-free environment.

3 But that is only the beginning. Other countries, including China, Taiwan and South Korea, and certain U.S. states are creating their own "green" or RoHS-like legislation. That means RoHS compliance must become an integral part of a designer's development process, with RoHS checks at each step: concept, development, prototype, first builds and volume production.

4 Major companies will run the gamut from finding component databases of qualified green components to taking due care to prove compliance and developing processes that allow for the higher-temperature requirements of Pb-free manufacturing. And for designers, those are just the tip of the iceberg. A host of technical and reliability issues remain to be sorted out in Pb-free board processing and soldering.

5 What it comes down to is what Ken Stanvick, senior vice president at Design Chain Associates, calls a lack of 'tribal knowledge' on design RoHS-compliant systems. 'We had a great tribal knowledge when it came to dealing with leaded systems, but we haven't built up that same amount of knowledge for Pb-free,' he said. 'Every problem will be blamed on Pb-free until it's been worked out. We need to figure out tests that replicate more of the environment and different stresses that we're going to see in this new system.'

6 Manny Marcano, president and CEO of EMA Design Automation Inc. (Rochester, N.Y.), cited the impact of parts obsolescence, including the need to redesign older products and the resultant emphasis on component engineering at the expense of conceptual design. A key challenge is identifying RoHS design specifications as early as possible in the design process, he said.

7   But even before they get to that point, designers must understand whether they are designing a fully compliant product or one that's subject to some exemptions, said Robert Chinn, director for consultant firm PRTM (Mountain View, Calif.). 'This affects their design parameters,' he said. 'Previously, they looked at components based on size, performance, electrical parameters, features and functionality. Now they have to add on a new constraint, revolving around environmental compliance: Is it RoHS 6-compliant or is it RoHS 5-compliant?' (RoHS 6 components eliminate all six of the banned substances, while RoHS 5 models, because of exemptions, still contain lead.)

8   If designers do not take RoHS seriously, any country that can prove a product does not comply can levy fines against the vendor. That can cost market share, Marcano said, since noncompliant companies become non-competitive. And then, not being prepared can mean belatedly diverting resources to RoHS compliance, causing missed market opportunities.

9   But many industry observers believe smaller and medium-size companies will continue to be complacent about the RoHS transition until some major company is cited for non-compliance. 'When that happens, there will be an earthquake throughout the industry, and it will wake up every design engineer,' said Steve Schultz, director of strategic planning and communications at Avnet Logistics and program manager for the distributor's compliance efforts for RoHS in the Americas.

10 'The product developer's RoHS concerns center on the fear of lost revenue – from a product ban, a customer who demands a RoHS-compliant product that the company doesn't have, or competition', said Harvey Stone, managing director for consultancy GoodBye Chain Group (Colorado Springs, Colo.). 'With price, quality and service being relatively equal, a savvy customer is going to choose a RoHS-compliant product,' he said.

11 Meanwhile, designers are looking over their shoulders at several other – and potentially stricter – environmental regulations in the pipeline. These include the EU's Registration, Evaluation and Authorization of Chemicals legislation, which could restrict the use of thousands of chemicals, and its Energy-using Products (EuP) directive, which will initially target energy-efficiency requirements.

Questions 14–17

Look at the following people and the list of statements below.

Match each person with the correct statement.

Write the correct letter A–G in boxes 14–17 on your answer sheet.

14 Manny Marcano

15 Harvey Stone

16 Steve Shultz

17 Ken Stanvick

List of Statements

A   believes that the EU directive requires no action

B   claims that old products need to be redesigned

C   claims that customers will want a RoHS compliant product

D   states that many products will be RoHS exempt

E   is involved in planning and communications

F   predicts that design engineers will like RoHS

G   claims that more knowledge about Pb-free systems is needed

---

Questions 18–24

Complete the summary using the list of words A–P below.

Write the correct letter A–P in boxes 18–24 on your answer sheet.

The EU has banned the use of six materials that are **18** .... to the environment. This means that if designers do not meet the Restriction of Hazardous Substances (RoHS) directive, sales will **19** .... Similar legislation is being put together around the world, which indicates that RoHS compliance needs to become a **20** .... part of a designer's development process. RoHS checks at every step from concept to mass production is also a necessity. But **21** .... technical and reliability problems remain to be **22** .... Previously, the performance etc. of components were **23** .... , but now a new **24** .... needs to be taken into account: environmental compliance.

A requirement	E big	I variety	M idea
B friendly	F basic	J decline	N small
C hostile	G insignificant	K solved	O recognised
D increase	H numerous	L important	P need

Questions 25–27

Do the following statements agree with the information in Reading Passage 2?

In boxes 25–27 on your answer sheet write

TRUE	*if the statement agrees with the information*
FALSE	*if the statement contradicts the information*
NOT GIVEN	*if there is no information about the statement*

25 Countries can impose fines on the sellers of products that do not comply with RoHS.

26 Smaller companies are taking the changeover to RoHS seriously.

27 The Energy-using directive will be introduced in the very near future.

Before you check your answers to Reading Passage 2, go on to page 52.

Further practice for Reading Passage 2

The questions below will help you make sure that you have chosen the correct answers for questions 14–24 in Reading Passage 2.

Matching names and statements

Look at questions 14–17 and answer the following:

1   Is it possible to use the same
technique as in classification?   Yes/No

2   Is it easier to see the names when
you box them?   Yes/No

3   Which words from each statement **A–G** can
you use to scan between the boxes?

A   ....

....

B   ....

....

C   ....

....

D   ....

....

E   ....

....

F   ....

....

G   ....

....

Summary completion

*Look at questions 18–24 and put the words **A–P** into the following groups.*

Adjectives: ....

....

Nouns: ....

....

Verbs: ....

....

Word type

Decide what type of word is needed for each gap.

18   ....

19   ....

20   ....

21   ....

22   ....

23   ....

24   ....

Checklist questions 18–24

Circle Yes/No.

18   If the materials have been banned,
are they environmentally good?   Yes/No

19   If the directive is not met, will
something positive happen?   Yes/No

20   If the legislation is everywhere,
is compliance essential?   Yes/No

21   Is there more than one problem?   Yes/No

22   Is the word *solved* related to
the word *problems*?   Yes/No

23   In the past was the performance
of components significant?   Yes/No

24   Is compliance something that is
unnecessary?   Yes/No

Now check your answers to these exercises. When you have done so, decide whether you wish to change any of your answers to Reading Passage 2. Then check your answers to Reading Passage 2.

Reading Passage 3

*You should spend about 20 minutes on **Questions 28–40**, which are based on Reading Passage 3 on the following pages.*

Questions 28–33

Reading Passage 3 has seven paragraphs **A–G**.

*Choose the correct heading for paragraphs **A** and **C–G** from the list of headings below.*

*Write the correct number, **i–ix**, in boxes **28–33** on your answer sheet.*

List of Headings
i   Some criticisms of video-conferencing
ii   The future of conferencing by video
iii   The transmission of education to remote areas
iv   The first stages of video-conferencing
v   The necessity of having two TVs
vi   How video-conferencing can benefit organizations
vii   How video-conferencing became more accessible to the general public
viii   The various pieces of equipment needed
ix   The lack of exploitation of video-conferencing in education

28 Paragraph A

Example	*Answer*
Paragraph **B**	*vii*

29 Paragraph C

30 Paragraph D

31 Paragraph E

32 Paragraph F

33 Paragraph G

Seeing the future in with video-conferencing

A   Video-conferencing (or Video tele-conferencing–VTC) as a means of communication intra- and inter-business has essentially been possible since the dawn of television. But the early systems, first demonstrated in 1968, were in fact so prohibitively expensive and of such poor picture quality that they were not viable applications for general public use.

B   However, in the 1980s, digital telephone networks like ISDN began to proliferate, so that by the 1990s the decrease in cost brought the equipment necessary for video-conferencing within the reach of the masses. The 1990s also saw the arrival of IP (Internet Protocol) based video-conferencing with more efficient video compression technologies being introduced, thus permitting desktop, or personal computer (PC)-based video-conferencing. VTC had come on the scene in a big way as free services, web plugins and software, such as NetMeeting, and MSN Messenger, Skype and others brought cheap, albeit low-quality, VTC to the public at large.

C   Video-conferencing has been disparaged for the lack of eye-contact that can affect the efficacy of the medium and for the fact that participants can be camera conscious. But these obstacles

are not insurmountable. The size of modern televisions along with the vast improvement in picture quality as a result of the arrival of the digital age has enhanced the potential of the latest video-conferencing equipment, going somewhat towards solving the former problem. Early studies by Alphonse Chapanis found that the addition of video hindered rather than improved communication. However, as with video and sound recording of meetings, interviews etc, awareness of the presence of the techology diminishes with time to the point that its presence is not felt. A further drawback common to all technology is the ever present possibility of technical hitches. But in the end video-conferencing is no different from any electronic device like a PC or a telephone and so in time, any problems will be ironed out.

D Conferencing by video has enhanced the performance of different organizations through its efficiency and effectiveness, saving both time and money for businesses and, in this carbon-conscious age, by the reduction in the environmental cost of business travel from one corner of the world to another. These apart, video-conferencing has an immediacy that is difficult to challenge. It is now essential in any work situation where organizations with employees on different sites or in different parts of the globe can contact each other rapidly. Like a telephone line permanently connected it is easy to dial up a colleague in seconds anywhere in the world.

E And what about the equipment? The equipment for video-conferencing is relatively straightforward to use. It has, in fact, been commonplace in the news media for a number of years as corporations have broadcast live from the back of a truck or van in news

hotspots around the world. Two ISDN lines are needed at each location: one for video output and the other for video input; a high quality camera with omnidirectional micrphones or micophones which can be hand-held, clipped on or central are required; and for data transfer a LAN is also needed. And, of course, a televison screen at each end is essential.

F The potential use of video-conferencing in the educational field has yet to be fully exploited. In this day and age when academic institutions are supposed to be more revenue conscious and much more flexible, video-conferencing could be employed to bring business into the educational field and vice versa. The system can also be used to take expertise anywhere in the world. It is no longer necessary for experts to travel vast distances for conferences or to teach. In certain areas, say remote islands like the Outer Hebrides in Scotland or the Cape Verde Islands off West Africa, where it may be difficult to find teachers in specialist subjects like languages, video-conferencing is a perfect way to bring education within the reach of everyone. Video-conferencing is certainly not a panacea for every problem, not an end in itself, but a useful tool that can complement rather than supplant existing teaching methods.

G Like the electronic or smart whiteboard, whose introduction in the classroom has met with resistance, video-conferencing may take some time to become mainstream, if ever. But, perhaps with the mounting concern about our carbon footprint, the environment will ultimately be the biggest spur. A sobering thought is whether classrooms and offices of the future will consist solely of TV screens.

Questions 34–36

Choose the correct letter A, B, C or D.

Write your answers in boxes 34–36 on your answer sheet.

34 Video-conferencing was not common initially because of

    A the cost and poor image quality.
    B poor advertising and marketing.
    C the lack of skilled technicians.
    D constant electronic failures.

35 Video-conferencing became more practical on personal computers once

    A the Internet became more widespread.
    B the picture quality became perfect.
    C the software became free for the general public.
    D video compression technology worked better.

36 Video-conferencing has been attacked for

    A several problems that cannot be solved.
    B the lack of large TV screens.
    C there not being direct eye contact.
    D the failure of new digital technology.

Questions 37–39

Choose THREE letters A–F.

Write your answers in boxes 37–39 on your answer sheet.

NB Your answers may be given in any order.

*Which **THREE** of the following statements are true of video-conferencing?*

    A It is cost-effective for businesses to use.

    B Operating VC equipment is not complicated.

    C It will solve many problems in the classroom.

    D More people now have the necessary skills to use video-conferencing.

    E Modern equipment rarely breaks down.

    F People in remote areas can have expertise taken to them.

Question 40

Choose the correct letter A, B, C or D.

Write your answer in box 40 on your answer sheet.

40 The writer concludes that the success of video-conferencing in the classroom

    A is less likely than that of the whiteboard.
    B will certainly be short-lived.
    C may be linked to many unknown factors.
    D may finally depend on the environment.

Before you check your answers to Reading Passage 3, go on to pages 57–58.

Further practice for Reading Passage 3

The questions below will help you make sure that you have chosen the correct answers for questions **34–40** in Reading Passage 3.

Multiple choice questions

Question 34

*Look at **Question 34** and answer the following:*

1   Does the word *initially* relate to a heading **i–ix** above?

   ....

2   Look at the stem and the alternatives A–D. Which gives a cause and which gives an effect?

   ....

3   Where in the paragraph is a cause or effect given?

   ....

4   Which linking words are used to show the relationship between cause and effect?

   ....

5   Are the words *advertising, technicians, electronic* in the paragraph?

   ....

Question 35

*Look at **Question 35** and answer the following:*

1   Which heading in the list **i–ix** does the stem relate to? Look at the word *more*.

   ....

2   Turn the alternatives into questions and answer the questions:

   a   Did the Internet make VC more practical on PCs?

   ....

b   Did the perfection of the picture quality make VC more practical on PCs?

   ....

c   Did the software becoming free make VC more practical on PCs?

   ....

d   Did video compression technology have an effect?

   ....

3   Does the word *efficient* in the paragraph relate to 'worked better'?

   ....

4   Which gives a cause and which gives an effect, the stem or the alternatives A–D?

   ....

Question 36

*Look at **Question 36** and answer the following:*

1   Which heading in the list **i–ix** does the word *attack* relate to?

   ....

2   Which word in the passage does *attack* relate to?

   ....

3   Which two of the alternatives are not given? Which one is false?

   ....

Finding true statements

This type of question is like *True/False/Not Given* questions combined with multiple choice questions.

Questions 37–39

Look at all the statements A–F.

1   Which paragraphs do the following words relate to, if any?

classroom	....
equipment	....
skills	....
remote areas	....
business	....

    ....

2   Choose the correct alternative for each statement:

    A   Is there any information about saving money?   Yes/No

    B   Is there a statement about using VC easily?   Yes/No

    C   Is information given about solving many classroom problems?   Yes/No

    D   Does the passage say clearly that people now have these skills?   Yes/No

    E   Does the passage mention how often the equipment breaks down?   Yes/No

    F   Does video-conferencing benefit people in remote areas?   Yes/No

Global multiple choice question

Question 40

*Look at **Question 40** and answer the following:*

1   Is the answer in the last paragraph?   Yes/No

2   Does the word *perhaps* show the writer is certain?   Yes/No

3   Is the comparison of the VC with the whiteboard negative?   Yes/No

Now check your answers to these exercises. When you have done so, decide whether you wish to change any of your answers to Reading Passage 3. Then check your answers to Reading Passage 3.

Writing   Academic Writing   60 minutes

WRITING TASK 1

You should spend about 20 minutes on this task.

The tables and pie chart show in percentage terms the results of a survey of a new shopping complex in Auckland, New Zealand.

Summarize the information by selecting and reporting the main features, and make comparisons where relevant.

Write at least 150 words.

Shops

Shoppers	Very satisfied	Satisfied	Dissatisfied	No Comment
Male	17	45	20	18
Female	34	37	20	9

Restaurants

Shoppers	Very satisfied	Satisfied	Dissatisfied	No Comment
Male	25	55	5	15
Female	27	32	21	20

Design

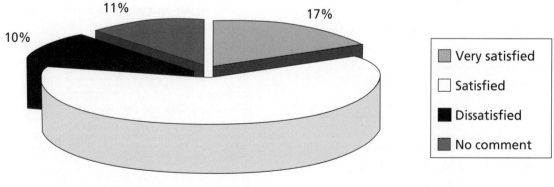

Before you write your answer to Task 1, go to page 60.

Further practice for Writing Task 1

When you are looking at data, remember to look for an overview and any noticeable features. Also think about what comparisons you can make.

1 *Look at Task 1. Decide which alternative in the questions a–h below is correct and write a sentence. Be careful with singular and plural.*

a Does the pie chart show that 'the overwhelming' or 'a small' majority of both sexes approved of the design?

....

....

b Did a greater proportion of women than men or more men than women dislike the restaurants?

....

....

c Did customers express their general satisfaction or dissatisfaction with the complex?

....

....

d Were there more men than women or not as many men as women, who made no comment about the shops?

....

....

e Did equal or unequal numbers of both sexes say they were unhappy with the shops?

....

....

f Do the data show the approval or disapproval rating of various aspects of a new shopping centre in Auckland, New Zealand?

....

....

g Were only 5 per cent of males displeased or pleased with the restaurants compared to 21 per cent of the females?

....

....

h Is it significant that the restaurants received a less or more positive rating overall among men than among women?

....

....

2 *Match the features i–iv below to the sentences in 1 above.*

i   an introduction

ii   an overview

iii a comparison

iv   a noticeable feature

3 *Add the data below to the end of the appropriate statements a–h you have written for 1 above.*

1 with 62 indicating their approval, 17 per cent being very satisfied, only 10 per cent dissatisfied and 11 per cent offering no comment.

2 80 per cent among male shoppers and only 59 per cent among females.

3 (18 per cent and 9 per cent, respectively).

4 with 20 per cent of males and females disapproving.

4 *Write your own answer to Task 1, adding the following linking words where appropriate.*

for example	as regards
generally speaking	overall
by contrast	however
it is clear that	by comparison

You may use some of the sentences or phrases above. When you have finished, compare your answer with the authentic student answer in the key on page 137.

Is your answer to Task 1 an appropriate length and have you used appropriate paragraphs?

WRITING TASK 2

You should spend about 40 minutes on this task.

Write about the following topic:

> *The world has seen an enormous increase in flights for leisure, business and commercial purposes around the world over recent years.*
>
> *What do you think are the main advantages and disadvantages of such flights?*
>
> *Do you think flights should be taxed more?*

Give reasons for your answer and include any relevant examples from your own knowledge and experience.

Write at least 250 words.

Before you write your answer to Task 2, go on to pages 62 and 63.

Further practice for Writing Task 2

For Task 2, you need to express your ideas in paragraphs, which explain ideas by giving reasons and examples.

ever before	holiday
last few decades	flying
popular	business
commercial	bring benefits
drawbacks	flights

1   *Write an introduction for Task 2 on page 61 using the words in the box:*

....

....

....

....

2   *Paragraph 2*

Look at the notes in the table below. Choose column 2 about Leisure and Commerce, or column 3 about Leisure and Business, and write a paragraph using the linking words given.

	Leisure and Commerce	Leisure and Business
Benefit	leisure/practical	leisure/time-saving
	convenient/flexible	destination quicker
because	long distances	need a quick break
for example if …		
like	Singapore/New York	Paris/London
then	travelling easier	more time for holiday
Likewise (Benefit 2)	commercial	business world/
	straightforward	make money easily
as	products fresh	meet customers easily
like	fruit/vegetable	companies overseas
as a result	more variety	cost-effective
therefore	beneficial	economical

Begin: Travelling by air for leisure purposes is a very practical means of transport, because ....

....

....

....

....

....

....

....

3 Paragraph 3
Write your own notes for a disadvantage, e.g.
carbon production, and then write a paragraph.

because ....

....

....

For example, ...

....

....

If ... don't ... .

....

....

then ....

....

....

which ....

....

....

As a result ....

....

....

4 Paragraph 4
Do the following notes reflect your opinion?
If they do not, change them to write your own
paragraph.

definitely tax because dangerous;
travel more by train; holiday
closer to home; buy local produce
less harmful; use plane only when
necessary

....

....

....

....

....

....

....

Now finish writing your essay. When you have
finished, compare it to the authentic student
answer on page 138.

Speaking  11–14 minutes

PART 1   Introduction and interview (4–5 minutes)

In this part of the examination you will be asked questions about yourself and familiar topics.

> **EXAMPLE**
>
> **Animals**
> - What's your name?
> - Where do you come from?
> - What's your favourite animal? Why?
> - Do you like the same animal now as you did when you were younger?
> - What can you learn about a person from the animals they like?
> - Which animals are popular as pets in your country?

PART 2   Individual long turn (3–4 minutes)

> **Describe a special occasion for which you arrived late.**
>
> You should say:
>
> what occasion you were late for
> when it happened
> how you felt
>
> and explain why you were late.

You will have to talk about this topic for one to two minutes. You have one minute to think about what you are going to say. You can make some notes to help you if you wish.

Now look at the Further Practice section on page 65.

PART 3   Two-way discussion (4–5 minutes)

In this part of the exam, the examiner will discuss a topic with you. The topic is usually related in some way to the topic in Part 2, but the questions will be of a more abstract nature.

Punctuality

> *Example questions:*
>
> Do you think it is important to be punctual for appointments? Why? Why not?
> What do you think about people who are always late?
> Normally how do people make excuses when they are late?

The effects of technology

> *Example questions:*
>
> Do you think modern technology has made people lazy?
> What do you think about modern technology for young people/ old people?
> How has modern technology changed people's lives for the better?

Now look at the Further Practice section on page 65.

Further practice for Speaking

In the Speaking paper you need to react to the questions rather than show you are thinking.

PART 2

Always make very short notes and use them to guide you as you speak.

1 _Look at the frame below, which is an answer to Part 2 on page 64 given by a student. Are the words underlined here suitable notes for Part 2?_

I would like to talk about a time when I was late for a <u>job interview</u> <u>earlier</u> in the <u>year</u>. The appointment was at 11am and I had got up early, as I .... I set off by train several hours in advance; in fact, I caught the train before I needed to. Unfortunately, the <u>train stopped</u> just outside my destination, because .... I was becoming very <u>nervous</u> and was even worried about telephoning. I used my mobile to <u>leave</u> a <u>message</u> with the receptionist, but I was anxious .... .

When I eventually arrived at the <u>interview</u> I was very <u>uneasy</u> and <u>tense</u>, because I felt .... I .... but I needn't have been so panicky, because .... The appointment was <u>important</u>, because .... .

---

2 _Complete the answer using your own words and then compare your answer with the key._

PART 3

It is important to develop your answer just as in a paragraph by giving reasons and examples. Use the examiner's questions to help you. Use adjectives to attach your ideas to and then explain the adjectives.

Discussion topics

Look at the first two questions in Part 3 on page 64.

Question 1

Decide which adjectives are synonyms for important:

optional	crucial	trivial	vital
necessary	critical	unimportant	

Then give your opinion and (a) reason(s):

I personally believe that ....

is (crucial) .... ,

because ....

What's more, ...

....

....

Question 2

Decide which adjectives you can use to describe people who are always late:

irritating	annoying	rude	frustrating
soothing	relaxing	stressful	

Then give your opinion and (a) reason(s):

I find people who are always late ....

...., because ....

....

and .... and so

....

Now practise the questions and answers in Part 3 with a partner.

Listening  approximately 30 minutes

Section 1   Questions 1–10

Complete the notes below.

Write **NO MORE THAN THREE WORDS AND/OR A NUMBER** *for each answer.*

Example	Answer
Purpose	placing an <u>advertisement</u>

Laptop for Sale

Condition	<u>Almost new</u>
Weight	**1** ....
Make	Allegro
Memory	**2** ....
Screen	**3** ....
Touch pad but with cordless mouse	
Number of ports	<u>Two</u>
Battery lasts	**4** ....
Latest programmes	Not **5** ....

Extras

Web cam	
Printer with	**6** ....
Smart case	
Price	**7** ....

Contact details

Name:	David **8** ....
E-mail address:	DIB_7791@hotmail.com
Mobile number:	**9** ....
Advert placed:	**10** ....

Stop the recording when you hear 'That is the end of Section 1'.
Before you check your answers to Section 1 of the test, go on to page 67.

Further practice for Listening Section 1

To help you predict the answers, think of a range within which the answer will occur. Put yourself in the position of the person giving the information: the seller of the laptop.

*Look at **Questions 1–7** on page 64 and choose the correct letter **a–c**.*

1   The weight of the laptop is likely to be in

   a   mg

   b   g

   c   kg

2   The memory is likely to be in

   a   MB (megabytes)

   b   KB (kilobytes)

   c   GB (gigabytes)

3   The size of the screen is likely to be in

   a   m

   b   cm

   c   mm

4   The battery life is likely to be in

   a   days

   b   hours

   c   minutes

5   Modern laptops are now likely to

   a   be wireless

   b   have lots of wires

   c   be waterproof

6   Which two extra pieces of equipment is the seller likely to include with the printer?

   a   headphones

   b   a mobile

   c   a scanner

7   What is the likely price for a used laptop in good condition with the extra equipment?

   a   at least £1000.

   b   more than £500.

   c   no more than £300.

Now check your answers to these exercises. When you have done so, listen again to Section 1 of the test and decide whether you wish to change any of your answers. Then check your answers to Section 1 of the test.

Section 2   Questions 11–20

Questions 11 and 12

Complete the sentences below.

*Write **NO MORE THAN THREE WORDS** for each answer.*

11 In the Club, there are nine ....

12 The main purpose of the Open Day is to give a .... of the premises.

Questions 13–15

Complete the table below.

*Write **NO MORE THAN TWO WORDS** for each answer.*

Name	Role
Sean Bond	to supervise equipment
Margaret Lloyd	to **13** ....
James Todd	to **14** ....
Edward Marks	to **15** ....

Questions 16–18

Which floor contains which amenities?

*Choose from **A–F**.*

A	storerooms
B	therapy rooms
C	offices
D	study area
E	cafeteria
F	lecture theatre

16 Ground floor   ....

17 First floor   ....

18 Second floor   ....

Questions 19 and 20

Complete the table below.

*Write **NO MORE THAN TWO WORDS AND/OR A NUMBER** for each answer.*

Programme	Number	Time of chat with trainers
Counselling	**19**	Saturday 10 am
Yoga etc	9	**20** .... pm

Stop the recording when you hear 'That is the end of Section 2.' Now check your answers.

Section 3   Questions 21–30

Complete the form below.

Write NO MORE THAN THREE WORDS AND/OR A NUMBER for each answer.

Joint Presentation
Self-evaluation Form

Title: The application of robotics in a non-industrial setting

Date: 21 ....

Insert your names and comments on the following aspects of the presentation.

	Mark	**Anna**	**Suggestions: Tutor**
General impression	worked well	not thorough or **22** .... enough	no comment
Hand-outs	**23** .... looking	the best part	reduce by **24** ....
Middle of presentation	power-point slides not in **25**	overestimated **26**	more practice with the equipment
Aims and objectives	very focused	clearly **27**	no comment
Delivery	performance was **28**	difficult to coordinate speaking and presenting	needs the **29** ....
Score	six	**30**	

Stop the recording when you hear 'That is the end of Section 3'.
Before you check your answers to Section 3 of the test, go on to page 70.

Further practice for Listening Section 3

In this Section, you hear three people talking with each other about an academic subject. You need to understand how information in a table fits together.

1 *Look at the table for* **Questions 21–30** *and answer the following questions.*

  a Are words like *overall, taken as a whole* associated with the word *general*?

  ....

  b To give an impression, do you often say *I think ..., I feel ... , my impression is ...*?

  ....

  c Does the word *thorough* mean *careless* or *thoughtful* or *systematic*?

  ....

  d Is the word *looking* related to appearance or attitude?

  ....

  e Which reduces a text more: reducing it **by** a third or **to** a third?

  ....

  f Is the problem with the slides likely to be the order or the colour?

  ....

  g Does *overestimated* mean *rated too highly* or *considered worthless*?

  ....

  h Can *score* mean *mark*?

  ....

2 *Expand the information in the table using words from* **a–h** *above.*

  22 General impression: Overall, Mark thought that the presentation went well, but when Anna spoke she thought that the presentation was not systematic or thorough enough.

23/24 Hand-outs: ....

....

....

....

....

....

25/26 Middle of presentation: ....

....

....

....

....

27 Aims and objectives: ....

....

....

....

....

28/29 Delivery: ....

....

....

....

....

....

30 Score: ....

....

....

....

....

Now check your answers to these exercises. When you have done so, listen again to Section 3 of the test and decide whether you wish to change any of your answers. Then check your answers to Section 3 of the test.

Section 4   Questions 31–40

Questions 31–33

Choose the correct letter A, B or C.

31 The local business people who had approached the Centre had all encountered

    A enormous problems.
    B few problems.
    C many obstacles.

32 The main focus of the Centre is now

    A large national companies.
    B technology companies.
    C businesses that have just started up.

33 Snapshot research was carried out

    A over the Internet.
    B by telephone.
    C by personal contact.

Questions 34 and 35

Answer the questions below.

*Write **NO MORE THAN THREE WORDS AND/OR A NUMBER** for each answer.*

34 How much higher are local business rents compared to those nationally?

    ....

35 How many local businesses close a year after they have started working with the Centre?

    ....

Questions 36–40

Complete the table below.

*Write **NO MORE THAN THREE WORDS** for each answer.*

Size of business	Companies	Help being given
Start-ups	O-foods	improving the 36 .... turnaround
	Innovations	support to attract business partners and achieve 37 ....
Small	Sampsons Ltd	business 38 ....
	Vintage Scooter	product monitoring scheme after sales customer service
Medium	Build Ltd	extension of 39 ....
	Jones Systems	conflict management and 40 ....

Stop the recording when you hear 'That is the end of Section 4.'
Now check your answers to Section 4 of the test.

Reading   Academic Reading   60 minutes

Reading Passage 1

*You should spend about 20 minutes on **Questions 1–13**, which are based on Reading Passage 1 below.*

CAVES

1 Caves are natural underground spaces, commonly those into which man can enter. There are three major types: the most widespread and extensive are those developed in soluble rocks, usually limestone or marble, by underground movement of water; on the coast are those formed in cliffs generally by the concentrated pounding of waves along joints and zones of crushed rock; and a few caves are formed in lava flows, where the solidified outer crust is left after the molten core has drained away to form rough tunnels, like those on the small basalt volcanoes of Auckland.

2 Limestone of all ages, ranging from geologically recent times to more than 450 million years ago, is found in many parts of New Zealand, although it is not all cavernous. Many caves have been discovered, but hundreds still remain to be explored. The most notable limestone areas for caves are the many hundreds of square kilometres of Te Kuiti Group (Oligocene) rocks from Port Waikato south to Mokau and from the coast inland to the Waipa Valley – especially in the Waitomo district; and the Mount Arthur Marble (upper Ordovician) of the mountains of north-west Nelson (fringed by thin bands of Oligocene limestone in the valleys and near the coast).

3 Sedimentary rocks (including limestone) are usually laid down in almost horizontal layers or beds which may be of any thickness, but most commonly of 5–7.5 cm. These beds may accumulate to a total thickness of about a hundred metres. Pure limestone is brittle, and folding due to earth movements causes cracks

along the partings, and joints at angles to them. Rain water percolates down through the soil and the fractures in the underlying rocks to the water table, below which all cavities and pores are filled with water. This water, which is usually acidic, dissolves the limestone along the joints and, once a passage is opened, it is enlarged by the abrasive action of sand and pebbles carried by streams. Extensive solution takes place between the seasonal limits of the water table. Erosion may continue to cut down into the floor, or silt and pebbles may build up floors and divert stream courses. Most caves still carry the stream that formed them.

4 Caves in the softer, well-bedded Oligocene limestones are typically horizontal in development, often with passages on several levels, and frequently of considerable length. Gardner's Gut, Waitomo, has two main levels and more than seven kilometres of passages. Plans of caves show prominent features, such as long, narrow, straight passages following joint patterns as in Ruakuri, Waitomo, or a number of parallel straights oriented in one or more directions like Te Anaroa, Rockville. Vertical cross sections of cave passages may be tall and narrow following joints, as in Burr Cave, Waitomo; large and ragged in collapse chambers, like Hollow Hill, Waitomo (233m long, 59.4m wide, and 30.48m high); low and wide along bedding planes, as in Luckie Strike, Waitomo; or high vertical water-worn shafts, like Rangitaawa Shaft (91m). Waitomo Caves in the harder, massive Mount Arthur Marble (a metamorphosed limestone) are mainly vertical in development, many reaching several hundred metres, the deepest known being Harwood Hole, Takaka (370m).

5 The unique beauty of caves lies in the variety of mineral encrustations which are found sometimes completely covering walls, ceiling, and floor. Stalactites (Gk. *stalaktos*, dripping) are pendent growths of crystalline calcium carbonate (calcite) formed from solution by the deposition of minute quantities of calcite from percolating ground water. They are usually white to yellow in colour, but occasionally are brown or red. Where water evaporates faster than it drips, long thin *straws* are formed which may reach the floor or thicken into *columns*. If the source of water moves across the ceiling, a thin *drape*, very like a stage curtain, is formed. Helictites are stalactites that branch or curl. Stalagmites (Gk. *stalagmos*, that which dripped) are conical or gnarled floor growths formed by splashing, if the water drips faster than it evaporates. These may grow toward the ceiling to form columns of massive proportions. Where calcite is deposited by water spreading thinly over the walls or floor, *flowstone* is formed and pools of water may build up their edges to form narrow walls of *rimstone*. Gypsum (calcium sulphate) is a white cave deposit of many crystal habits which are probably dependent on humidity. The most beautiful form is the gypsum flower which extrudes from a point on the cave wall in curling and diverging bundles of fibres like a lily or orchid.

Questions 1–3

Complete the summary.

Choose ONE WORD ONLY from the passage for each answer.

Write your answers in boxes 1–3 on your answer sheet.

There are several **1** .... of caves with the most common and largest being located in limestone or marble. Coastal caves are created in cliffs usually by waves. In lava flows, the solidified outer crusts that remain once the molten core has drained away also form **2** .... Limestone is to be found all over New Zealand, but not all of it contains caves. While many caves are known, there are large numbers that have yet to be uncovered. The main **3** .... for limestone caves are Te Kuiti Group rocks.

Questions 4–8

Complete the flow-chart.

Choose ONE WORD ONLY from the passage for each answer.

Write your answers in boxes 4–8 on your answer sheet.

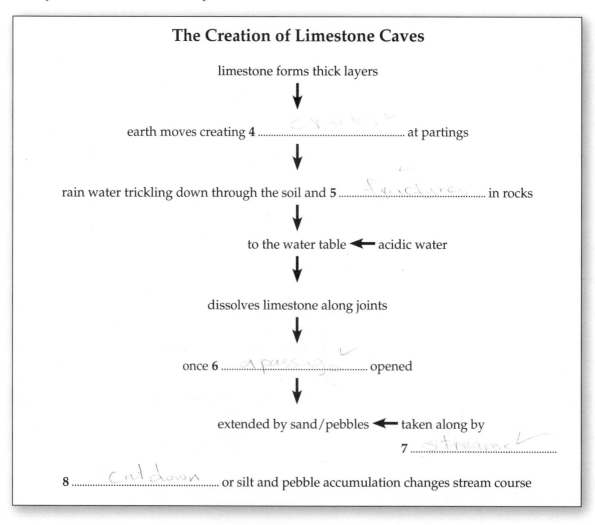

The Creation of Limestone Caves

limestone forms thick layers

↓

earth moves creating **4** .... at partings

↓

rain water trickling down through the soil and **5** .... in rocks

↓

to the water table ◀ acidic water

↓

dissolves limestone along joints

↓

once **6** .... opened

↓

extended by sand/pebbles ◀ taken along by **7** ....

8 .... or silt and pebble accumulation changes stream course

Questions 9 and 10

*Choose **TWO** letters A–E.*

*Write the correct letter **A–E** in boxes **9 and 10** on your answer sheet.*

NB Your answers may be given in either order.

*Which **TWO** of the following features of caves in the softer limestones are mentioned in the text?*

    A   they are often long

    B   they are all at least 7.2km long

    C   most of them are vertical

    D   they only ever have one passage

    E   they are characteristically horizontal

Questions 11–13

Do the following statements agree with the information in Reading Passage 1?

*In boxes **11–13** on your answer sheet write*

TRUE   *if the statement agrees with the information*
FALSE   *if the statement contradicts the information*
NOT GIVEN *if there is no information about the statement*

11 The limestone found in New Zealand is more than 450 million years old.

12 Stalactites are more often white to yellow than brown or red.

13 Stalagmites never grow very large.

Before you check your answers to Reading Passage 1, go on to pages 76 and 77.

Further practice for Reading Passage 1

Flow-charts are often written in note form.

Look at Questions 4–8 and answer the following questions:

Question 4

1   Is this something to do with cause and effect?

....

2   Is the movement of the earth causing something like holes or gaps?

....

Question 5

1   Is question 5 related to question 4?

....

2   Is the missing word a synonym of 4?

....

Question 6

1   Is this something to do with a bigger version of the words in 4 and 5?

....

2   Is the answer a noun with an article and an auxiliary verb?

....

Question 7

1   Is this something to do with water? (Look at 8)

....

2   In the process, is there likely to be just one thing or several of these things carrying the pebbles along?

....

Question 8

Is the other cause a physical process?

....

Look at Questions 11–13 and answer the following questions.

Question 11

Look at paragraph 2.

1   Is limestone found in New Zealand?

....

2   Is the limestone of one age only?

....

3   Does the question say: *The limestone found in New Zealand*?

....

4   Does the phrase mean *all* the limestone that is found in New Zealand?

....

Question 12

Look at paragraph 5.

1   Are the stalactites usually white in colour?

    ....

2   Are the stalactites occasionally brown or red?

    ....

3   Does the word *usually* refer to something
    that happens more often than the word
    occasionally?

    ....

Question 13

Look at paragraph 5.

1   Does the text mention the fact that
    stalagmites grow?

    ....

2   Does the word *massive* mean *small*?

    ....

3   Does the word *may* in the passage mean that
    they sometimes become massive?

    ....

4   Does the word *never* contradict the word
    may?

    ....

Now check your answers to these exercises. When you have done so, decide whether you wish to change any of your answers to Reading Passage 1. Then check your answers to Reading Passage 1.

Reading Passage 2

*You should spend about 20 minutes on **Questions 14–27**, which are based on Reading Passage 2 below.*

1 Left- or right-handed bath water? This seems a silly question, but it was the subject of a serious scientific investigation sponsored by the Daily Mail in 1965. The investigation showed that the direction water swirls down the plug-hole vortex depends on which side of the Equator you are.

2 As for homo sapiens, between 5 and 30% of the population are estimated to be left-handed, with more males than females, although in one test, 95% of foetuses were found to suck their right thumb in the womb. The general consensus of opinion is that left-handedness is determined by a dominant right cerebral hemisphere controlling the left side of the body, and vice versa. Hereditary factors have been ruled out. So too have earlier theories concerning the need for soldiers to shield their hearts, and the desirability of learning to use Stone Age tools and implements with the hand they were designed for, as well as Plato's idea that it all boiled down to which arm a baby was cradled with. However, the almost universal human preference for dextrality, or right-handedness, remains a mystery.

3 Prejudice against the left hand dates back to ancient times and is so entwined with religious beliefs and superstitions that it still exists today in everyday speech. *Sinister*, the Latin for *left hand*, means 'suggestive of evil' in English, while the French *gauche* is awkward, or clumsy. *Left* itself derives from Anglo Saxon *lef* (weak and fragile). The non-judgmental term *southpaw*, by contrast, originates from the Chicago baseball stadium where pitchers faced west, so the pitching arm of a left-hander is to the South.

4 Other negative terms include *pen pushers*, while a *left-handed compliment* is actually an insult. Thomas Carlyle, who described right-handedness as *the oldest institution in the world*, introduced the political concept of 'left' in his work on the French Revolution – in the 1789 Paris Assembly the nobles sat on the right, opposite the radicals.

5 Associations with luck also go back to early history. The ancient Greek and Roman augurs foretold the future from bird-flight. While the former faced North, with the propitious sunrise side to their right, the latter, before changing later, when *sinister* took on its ominous meaning, looked southward, so the left was for good omens.

6 Superstitions world-wide reflect this bias. In Morocco, as in many countries, an itchy left palm means losing money, and a twitching left eyelid denotes the death of a relative or sorrow, whereas the right side has felicitous indications. We throw salt over our left shoulder to thwart the demons creeping up on us, but bless with the right hand. One pours wine with this hand and passes it round the table clockwise, the direction of the sun.

7 Our relatives, the primates, appear to be ambidextrous, or able to use both hands, although gorillas have heavier left arms seemingly due to greater utilization. Aristotle observed that crabs and lobsters had larger right claws. Rats are 80% dextral, yet polar bears are believed to be left-pawed. Flat fish provide interesting data: in northern seas plaice and sole have their eyes and colour on the right side, but tropical halibut are the other way round. If this is to do with light and sun rotation, it may explain why Indian Ocean sole are reversed, but not why northern halibut are just as sinistral as their southern cousins. In the plant kingdom, honeysuckle is a rare example of a left-handed climber that twines anti-clockwise, or widdershins!

8 Although we live in a more tolerant age, not so long ago in the UK youngsters were forced to use their right hand, 'to learn the value of conformity' (A. N. Palmer), often resulting in the stuttering speech defects common in 'switched sinistrals' like George VI. In the 1950s the American psychiatrist Abram Blau accused left-handed children of infantile perversity and a stubborn refusal to accept dextrality.

9 Not all experts were so anti-sinistral, however. The 17th century Norfolk scholar Sir Thomas Browne wrote of the prejudices against left-handedness, but accepted that a small proportion of people would always be so and saw no reason to prevent them. Apart from being considered difficult, anti-social troublemakers, left-handers have also been thought to be artistic, creative and gifted.

10 Famous lefties include Leonardo da Vinci, Michelangelo, Benjamin Franklin, Bill Clinton, Joan of Arc, Lewis Carroll, Paul McCartney, Jimi Hendrix, Jean Genet, Beethoven and many others.

11 Finally, in defence of all sinistrals, if the left side of the body is really controlled by the right hemisphere of the brain, then left-handers are the only people in their right minds!

Questions 14–18

Choose the correct letter A, B, C or D.

Write your answers in boxes 14–18 on your answer sheet.

14   The direction of water going down the plug-hole

    A   is not related to where you are.
    B   is independent of the side of the Equator you are on.
    C   is linked to the side of the Equator you are on.
    D   was first discovered by the Daily Mail in the 1950s.

15   In determining left-handedness, hereditary factors are generally considered

    A   as important.
    B   as having no impact.
    C   as being a major influence.
    D   as being the prime cause.

16   The reason why

    A   almost everyone is right-handed is unknown.
    B   some people are right-handed is ambiguous.
    C   Plato worked out the mystery of left-handedness is not known.
    D   many people are right-handed is now clear.

17   The word 'southpaw' is

    A   an Anglo-Saxon term.
    B   not a negative term.
    C   suggestive of evil.
    D   a negative term.

18   The left was connected with

    A   being unclean by the Greeks.
    B   goodness by the French.
    C   fortune and bird-flight by many cultures.
    D   good fortune in ancient Greece and Rome.

Questions 19–22

Answer the questions below.

Choose NO MORE THAN TWO WORDS from the passage for each answer.

Write your answers in boxes 19–22 on your answer sheet.

19 Who was the originator of the political concept of left?

20 What did the ancient Romans use to predict the future?

21 What does an itchy palm in the left hand mean?

22 In which direction is wine passed round the table?

Questions 23–26

Complete each sentence with the correct ending A–G.

Write your answers in boxes 23–26 on your answer sheet.

23 Gorillas, unlike other primates,

24 Fish colour and eye position

25 Most plant climbers

26 In the past some experts

> A   appear to have been against left-handedness.
>
> B   are usually the same in both hemispheres.
>
> C   are apparently not always dependent on hemisphere.
>
> D   seem to have difficulty using both hands.
>
> E   looked on left-handedness with indifference.
>
> F   tend to grow clockwise rather that anti-clockwise.
>
> G   seem to use their left-hand more.

Question 27

Choose the correct letter A, B, C, D or E.

Write your answer in box 27 on your answer sheet.

Which of the following is the most suitable title for Reading Passage 2?

   A   Left-handedness and primates

   B   A defence of right-handedness

   C   A defence of left-handedness

   D   Left-handedness and good luck

   E   Left-handedness and bad luck

Before you check your answers to Reading Passage 2, go on to page 82.

Further practice for Reading Passage 2

To match sentence beginnings and endings, find the stem and put a box around the key words. Then try to match key words or synonyms from the endings with the stem.

Look at **Questions 23–26** and answer the following questions.

Question 23

Look at paragraph 7.

1   Can gorillas use both hands, i.e. are they ambidextrous?

   ....

2   Do gorillas seem to utilize their left arms more and make them more muscular?

   ....

3   If the left arms are muscular, are they likely to be heavier?

   ....

4   Is the ending D true about primates and therefore gorillas?

   ....

Question 24

Look at paragraph 7.

1   Does the passage compare fish colour and eye position in some way?

   ....

2   Is the comparison between fish in different seas, northern and southern?

   ....

3   Does the passage mention that the northern halibut is an exception?

   ....

4   Does the ending C show that there is possibly an exception to a rule?

   ....

Question 25

Look at paragraph 7.

1   Does the honeysuckle grow anti-clockwise as it climbs?

   ....

2   Is the honeysuckle a common example of a plant climbing anti-clockwise?

   ....

3   Do most climbers climb clockwise?

   ....

4   Does the honeysuckle coil as it grows?

   ....

Question 26

Look at paragraphs 8 and 9.

1   Does paragraph 8 give examples of experts being against left-handedness?

   ....

2   Does paragraph 9 state the same?

   ....

3   Does this mean that not all experts were against left-handedness?

   ....

4   Does the ending A mention being in favour of left-handedness?

   ....

Now check your answers to these exercises. When you have done so, decide whether you wish to change any of your answers to Reading Passage 2. Then check your answers to Reading Passage 2.

Reading Passage 3

*You should spend about 20 minutes on **Questions 28–40**, which are based on Reading Passage 3 below.*

PHYSICIAN, RULE THYSELF!

Professions and self-regulation

A When is an occupation a profession? There appears to be no absolute definition, but only different ways of looking at the issue, from historical, cultural, sociological, moral, political, ethical or philosophical viewpoints. It is often said that professions are elites who undertake specialized, selfless work, in accordance with ethical codes, and that their work is guaranteed by examination and a licence to practise. In return, however, they request exclusive control over a body of knowledge, freedom to practise, special rewards and higher financial and economic status.

B The public needs experts to offer them specialist advice, but because this advice is specialized they are not in a position to know what advice they need: this has to be defined in conversation with the professional. Professional judgement could be at odds with client satisfaction since the latter cannot then be "the chief measure of whether the professional has acted in a trustworthy fashion." Professional elites have negative potential: to exploit their power and prestige for economic goals; to allow the search for the necessary theoretical or scientific knowledge to become an end in itself; to lose sight of client well-being in the continuing fragmentation of specialist knowledge.

C Professions in different cultures are subject to different levels of state intervention, and are shaped by this. In England our relatively weak state and the organic growth of professional groups, many of them licensed by Royal Charter, means that regulation became an arrangement among elites. Similarly, in the US, where liberal market principles have had a free rein, academic institutions have had more influence than the state in the development of the professions. By contrast, in many European countries the state has defined and controlled the market for the professions since the late eighteenth and early nineteenth centuries. In all cases, the activities of the professions affect public interest, and so the state has a legitimate interest in them.

D In general, the higher the social status of a profession the greater the degree of public trust in it, and the more freedom to operate it enjoys. There are, however, certain features which appear to be common to most, if not all, professions. In addition to a specialised knowledge base, it appears that there is an agreed set of qualifications and experience which constitutes a licence to practise. There is also frequently an agreed title or form of address, coupled with a particular, often conservative, public image, and an accepted mode of dress. Standards are maintained mainly through self-regulatory bodies. Also, financial rewards may be increased through private practice.

E   Within different cultures, and at different times, the relative status of different professions may vary. For example, in Western Europe, the status of politicians has been in long-term decline since the middle of the twentieth century. Teachers would appear to have higher status in France and Italy than in the UK, where medicine and the law have traditionally been the 'elite professions'.

F   The higher a profession's social status the more freedom it enjoys. Therefore, an occupation wanting to maintain or improve its status will try to retain as much control as possible over its own affairs. As in so many other areas, socio-cultural change has affected the professions considerably in recent years. Market forces and social pressures have forced professionals to be more open about their modes of practice. In addition, information technology has enabled the public to become much better informed, and therefore more demanding. Moreover, developments in professional knowledge itself have forced a greater degree of specialisation on experts, who constantly have to retrain and do research to maintain their position.

G   Self-regulation then becomes an even more important thing for a profession to maintain or extend. But in whose interests? Is self-regulation used to enable a profession to properly practise without undue interference, or is it used to maintain the status of the profession for its own ends? Is it used to enable those with appropriate education and training to join the profession? Another question that needs to be answered is whether self-regulation restricts access so that the profession retains its social and economic privileges? Or again is it used to protect clients by appropriately disciplining those who have transgressed professional norms, or to protect the public image of the profession by concealing allegations that would damage it?

H   These are all questions which the medical profession in the UK has recently had to address, and which remain the subject of continuing debate. One thing is clear, however: the higher a profession's status, the better equipped it is to meet these challenges.

Questions 28–32

Reading Passage 3 has eight paragraphs **A–H**.

Which paragraph contains the following information?

*Write the correct letter **A–H** in boxes **28–32** on your answer sheet.*

28 how professionals have adjusted to socio-cultural developments

29 the typical characteristics that a profession has

30 the role that is played by governments in different countries

31 a description of the relationship between professionals and their clients

32 the fact that there is no clear definition of what a profession is

Questions 33–37

Complete the sentences.

*Choose **NO MORE THAN THREE WORDS** from the passage for each answer.*

*Write your answers in boxes **33–37** on your answer sheet.*

33 Professionals cannot always ensure that the .... given will satisfy the client.

34 Liberal market principles in the US have meant that the state has had less impact on the development of the professions than ....

35 An agreed set of qualifications and experience give professionals a ....

36 Over the past 50 years or so, the status of politicians has been in ....

37 There is a doubt as to whether .... is a mechanism to safeguard a profession's social and economic privileges.

Questions 38–40

Complete the table.

*Choose **NO MORE THAN TWO WORDS** from the passage for each answer.*

*Write your answers in boxes **38–40** on your answer sheet.*

Impact of socio-cultural change on professions

Factors	Implications
Various public influences	professionals 38 .... about work.
Modern technology	people more knowledgeable and so more 39 ....
Progress in professional knowledge	a greater degree of 40 .... needed

Before you check your answers to Reading Passage 3, go on to page 86.

Further practice for Reading Passage 3

Matching sentences is like matching paragraph headings. However, there may be one or more of the sentences which relate to part of a paragraph rather than a whole paragraph.

Choose True(T) or False(F) for the following sentences.

Question 28

Look at paragraph F.

1   The paragraph describes different
    ways professionals have changed.   T/F

2   The paragraph links the ways with
    phrases like *in addition, moreover.*   T/F

3   The word *how* means *way(s) by which.*   T/F

Question 29

Look at paragraph D.

1   The word *characteristics* is plural,
    meaning *more than one.*   T/F

2   There is more than one linking
    word meaning *in addition.*   T/F

3   The word *features* does not mean
    the same as *characteristics.*   T/F

Question 30

Look at paragraph C. Why is each statement below true?

1   *Different* and *countries* in the question mean
    there is more than one country.

    ....

    ....

2   The word *controlled* in the paragraph is
    related to the word *role.*

    ....

    ....

3   Words like *state intervention, shaped, regulation, licensed* etc. are connected with control.

    ....

    ....

Question 31

Look at paragraph B. Which statements are True(T)/ False(F)? Correct those which are false.

1   The word *client* is not related to the
    word *professional* in the paragraph.   T/F

2   The client/professional relationship
    is not explained in G.   T/F

3   The phrase *between professional
    and clients* explains the relationship.   T/F

Question 32

Look at paragraph A. Which statements are True(T)/ False(F)? Correct those which are false.

1   The question in the first sentence
    gives you a clue.   T/F

2   The second sentence confirms this:
    ... *no absolute definition.*   T/F

3   The whole paragraph is about the
    lack of clear definition.   T/F

Now check your answers to these exercises. When you have done so, decide whether you wish to change any of your answers to Reading Passage 3. Then check your answers to Reading Passage 3.

Writing   Academic Writing 60 minutes

WRITING TASK 1

You should spend about 20 minutes on this task.

The diagram below shows how rainwater is reused.

Summarize the information by selecting and reporting the main features, and make comparisons where relevant.

Write at least 150 words.

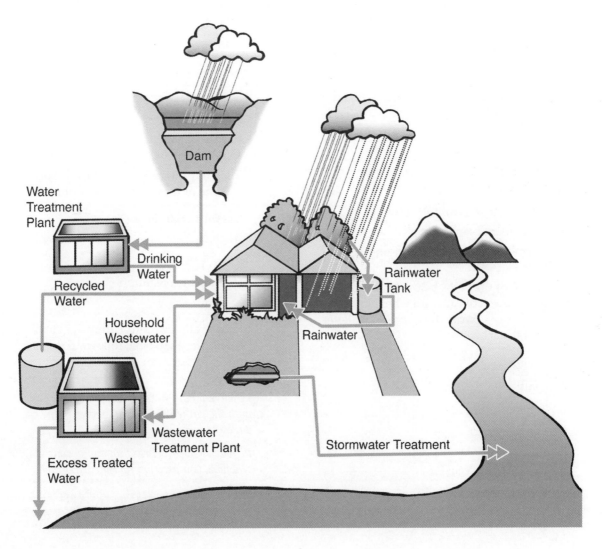

Before you write your answer to Task 1, go on to page 88.

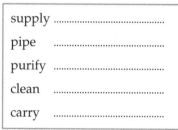

Further practice for Writing Task 1

Use the present simple and a mixture of active and passive verb forms for processes which are repeated.

Look at the diagram on page 87 and answer the following questions:

1 What is the best order to put the three stages below?

> **Stage A**
> household waste-water (treat)
> excess treated water (send to river)
> recycled water (send back to house)

> **Stage B**
> rain (fall)
> rain (collect/store in tank to water the garden)
> storm-water (send via drain to river)

> **Stage C**
> rain (fall)
> dam (collect/store)
> treatment plant (treat)
> drinking water (send to homes)

2 Which of the verbs below from **1** can you use in the active (a) and which in the passive (p)? Write the appropriate letter next to each verb.

send	....
fall	....
collect	....
store	....
treat	....

3 Match the following verbs with those in **2**:

supply	....
pipe	....
purify	....
clean	....
carry	....

4 What nouns can you make from the following verbs?

collect	....
store	....
recycle	....
treat	....
purify	....
supply	....

5 Write your own answer to Task 1. You may use some of these sentences or phrases:

> **Useful vocabulary**
>
> step, phase
>
> to produce drinking water/to make it fit for human consumption
>
> used to
>
> First of all, second(ly), third(ly), finally, then, after that, next, following that, once, before, after

When you have finished, compare your answer with the authentic student answer in the key on page 144.

Is your answer to Task 1 an appropriate length, and have you used appropriate paragraphs?

WRITING TASK 2

You should spend about 40 minutes on this task.

Write about the following topic:

>*Recent research has shown that media like the Internet and TV have a greater influence over people's lives than politicians.*
>
>*Which do you consider to be the greater influence?*

Give reasons for your answer and include any relevant examples from your own knowledge and experience.

Write at least 250 words.

Before you write your answer to Task 2, go on to pages 90–91.

Further practice for Writing Task 2

Look at the first two paragraphs of a model answer for Task 2 and answer the questions below.

> Politicians do, to a certain extent, have an impact on our lives. However, in my opinion, media like the Internet and TV have invaded every aspect of our lives. This has made it very difficult to spend a day without coming into contact with them, and so they now exert a much greater influence.
>
> The Internet is becoming more central to our lives than any other force including politicians, because it not only provides information, but it also helps people share their opinions. For example, if information about travelling by train or plane is required, the most convenient source is the Internet. Moreover, when an important event like an election occurs anywhere, people can express their opinions on the web before the information reaches other media like TV and radio. As a result, the Internet is now so potent that politicians are being forced to release pod-casts on line to try to harness its power.

1   *Look at the first paragraph and answer the following questions:*

   a   Does the introduction state an opinion as requested in the question?

   ....

   b   Does the introduction compare the two influences?

   ....

   c   Does the introduction copy the question?

   ....

2   *Look at the second paragraph and answer the following questions:*

   a   Does the first sentence use an adjective to give an opinion about the Internet?

   ....

   b   Does the first sentence give an effect of this opinion?

   ....

   c   Is the second sentence an example with an *if* clause?

   ....

   d   Is the third sentence a contrast of the previous sentence?

   ....

   e   Is the fourth sentence an effect the Internet has on politicians?

   ....

   f   Does the fourth sentence also give the purpose of politicians' use of the Internet?

   ....

3   *Write the linking words as they occur in sequence below:*

   Paragraph 1:...

   ....

   ....

   Paragraph 2:...

   ....

4 *Write a similar paragraph about TV. Use as many of the linking words in Paragraph 2 as you can.*

5 *Finish the essay in your own words. When you have finished writing your essay, use questions a–h below to check what you have written.*

a Is your answer divided into paragraphs?

....

b Have you written at least 150 words?

....

c Does each paragraph contain reasons and examples?

....

d Does your essay answer the question?

....

e Have you checked for mistakes?

....

f Have you used a range of vocabulary to avoid repetition?

....

g Have you used complex sentences?

....

h Can you give a heading to each paragraph you have written?

....

Now check your answer with the authentic student answer on page 145 in the key.

Speaking  11–14 minutes

PART 1   Introduction and interview (4–5 minutes)

In this part of the examination you will be asked questions about yourself and familiar topics.

> **EXAMPLE**
>
> **TV**
> - What is your name?
> - Where do you come from?
> - Tell me about TV in your country.
> - Do you watch a lot of TV?
> - What is your favourite programme?
> - Is television more important to you now than in the past?

PART 2   Individual long turn (3–4 minutes)

> **Describe an activity such as a hobby or sport you like doing.**
>
> You should say:
>
> what the activity is.
> when you started doing it
> what you like about the activity
>
> and explain why this activity is important for you.

You will have to talk about this topic for one to two minutes. You have one minute to think about what you are going to say. You can make some notes to help you if you wish.

Now look at the Further Practice section on page 93.

PART 3   Two-way discussion (4–5 minutes)

In this part of the exam, the examiner will discuss a topic with you. The topic is usually related in some way to the topic in Part 2, but the questions will be of a more abstract nature.

Purpose of skills in the modern world

> *Example questions:*
>
> What do you think are the most important skills for children to learn in the modern world? Why?
> Which skills do you think children should learn at school and which at home? Why?
> Do you think future generations will need to acquire new skills? What kind?

Skills and work

> *Example questions:*
>
> What role do you think skills play in the modern work place?
> Do you think the skills that people need nowadays have changed compared to the past?
> Why? Why not?
> What do you think has brought about these changes?

Now look at the Further Practice section on page 94.

Further practice for Speaking

In the exam, try to speak spontaneously and naturally. Do not learn models by heart, but learn phrases that can help you start sentences.

PART 2

1 *Complete the sentences below using your own words.*

a The .... I like doing most is ....

....

....

....

b The first time I did it was (last year) ....

....

....

....

c First of all, I enjoy ....

....

....

d Secondly, it is relaxing ....

....

....

e Another thing is ....

....

....

f I would say it is more important to me

....

....

....

g It's also valuable ....

....

....

h And so ....

....

....

2 *As in d, f and g in* **1** *above, use adjectives to help you develop ideas:*

... exciting, because ...; *or*

..., because ... exciting.

Try to use the following linking words: because, when, as, but, moreover etc.

3 *Are all of these verbs followed by a verb + -ing?*

like	be fond of	be keen on	enjoy
dislike	love	adore	

4 *Practise speaking with a partner for 1–2 minutes.*

PART 3

Learn to develop your answer to a question by saying at least three or four sentences.

1   *Below is a list of skills that are necessary for the modern world, with lists of beneficial effects. Underline the **least likely** benefit in each case. Add your own, if possible.*

> *Example*
>
> **a**   computer literacy: better job – better standard of living – happier – <u>more friends</u> – work more efficiently – more free time
>
> ....

b   flexibility/adaptability: more job choices – more varied life – better accommodation – more freedom – less stress

....

c   literacy and numeracy: more confident – more leisure time – better job prospects – more opportunities – better communication

....

d   speaking/on the telephone: more holidays – more friends – more contacts – happier life – better communication

....

e   socializing: more friends – learn to deal with people – fewer injuries – improve networking skills – more business – more enjoyable life

....

f   dealing with people: more successful – fewer money problems – more confident – more popular – solve problems easily

....

g   working in a team: more cooperative – promotion – more respect for others – no problems with managers

....

2   *Now explain your ideas about the beneficial effects of having the skill of computer literacy (**1a**) by beginning:*

If people are/someone is ....

....
....
....
....
....
....

Talk about the rest of the ideas by using the following language:

leads to	makes
if	and so
then	because

3   *Choose one of the skills in **1** and develop it using these phrases:*

If someone isn't ....

....
....
....

Moreover, unless ....

....
....

Workers also need to be .... ;

otherwise ....

....
....
....

4   *Which of the skills above do you think are more important nowadays compared to the past? Why?*

I think computer literacy is now crucial for everyone, because ... and so ...

Instead ... which meant ... and ...

But now ... and so ...

Practise asking and answering the questions in Part 3 with a partner.

TEST FOUR

Listening  approximately 30 minutes

Section 1   Questions 1–10

Questions 1–4

Choose the correct letter A, B or C.

> *Example*
>
>   How many types of membership are there?
>
>   **(A)** Two.
>   **B** Three.
>   **C** One.

1   How much is the life-time membership of the Society?

   A   £1,535.
   B   £1,935.
   C   £1,537.

2   How much does the ordinary membership cost per year?

   A   £293.
   B   £396.
   C   £193.

3   What are the opening times on week-days?

   A   9 am to 10 pm.
   B   10 am to 9 pm.
   C   10 am to 5 pm.

4   What is the arts programme at the Society like?

   A   limited.
   B   wide.
   C   interesting.

Questions 5–10

Complete the notes below.

*Write **NO MORE THAN TWO WORDS AND/OR A NUMBER** for each answer.*

Name	Margaret 5 ....
Address	55 6 ....
Postcode	7 ....
Work number	0207 895 2220 Extension 8 ....
Payment terms	by 9 ....
Guest restrictions	one per 10 ....

Stop the recording when you hear 'That is the end of Section 1.' Now check your answers.

Section 2   Questions 11–20

Questions 11 and 12

Choose TWO letters A–E.

What TWO changes to the organization of this year's festival are mentioned?

A   free parking

B   free refreshments

C   new uniforms

D   free concert

E   large tents

Questions 13–15

Complete the table below.

Write NO MORE THAN ONE WORD AND/OR A NUMBER for each answer.

Teams	Purpose	Meeting point	Time
Beach Team	pick up litter	Beach 13	8 am
Town Team	arrange 14	Village Hall	15 .... am

Questions 16–20

Choose the correct letter A, B or C.

16   What does the speaker say about the judges in the competitions?

A   Most people judging will have some experience.
B   None of the judges will have experience.
C   Every judge will be experienced.

17   The winner in each of the competitions will

A   be given vouchers.
B   be awarded a cash prize.
C   receive book-tokens.

18   The profits from the marathon will be given to the Children's Hospital to help

A   buy new specialist equipment.
B   decorate the hospital wards.
C   provide books for the children.

19   Wardens will be needed at the car park because

A   they helped organize the parking well last year.
B   the parking last year was disorganized.
C   they will be needed to collect parking fees.

20   Bags will be provided by the council

A   for all the rubbish.
B   only for food rubbish.
C   only for material that can be recycled.

Stop the recording when you hear 'That is the end of Section 2'. Before you check your answers, go on to page 97.

Further practice for Listening Section 2

Listening for information requires concentration on detail.

Listen to Section 2 again and correct the wrong information in each sentence. More than one answer may be possible.

Questions 11–15

11 People will be charged something for the concert.

....

....

12 People will have to pay a charge for the refreshments.

....

....

13 The Beach Team is to meet at the Beach Café.

....

....

14 The Town Team will set out chairs in the park.

....

....

15 The Town Team will meet earlier than the Beach Team.

....

....

Questions 16–20

16 All the judges are experienced.

....

....

17 The runners-up receive money as a prize.

....

....

18 The marathon profits will pay for specialist technicians.

....

....

19 The parking last year was well-organized.

....

....

20 The food will be put into the recycling bags.

....

....

Now check your answers to these exercises. When you have done so, listen again to Section 2 of the test and decide whether you wish to change any of your answers to Section 2. Then check your answers to Section 2 of the test.

Section 3   Questions 21–30

Questions 21–23

Choose the correct letter A, B or C.

21 In the practice exams, the students did

    A   two exams altogether.
    B   seven exams in total.
    C   eleven exams in total.

22 Adam thinks that essay papers are

    A   inappropriate for assessing theoretical medical knowledge.
    B   not good for assessing practical medical knowledge.
    C   suitable for testing theoretical medical knowledge.

23 Mary criticizes multiple-choice questions, because

    A   they require detailed instructions.
    B   they benefit women more than men.
    C   they favour men rather than women.

Questions 24 and 25

Choose TWO letters A–E.

Which two aspects of the role-play examination are mentioned?

    A   the rest stations

    B   24 test stations

    C   the recording

    D   the examiners

    E   the simulated patients

Questions 26–30

Complete the summary below.

*Write **NO MORE THAN TWO WORDS AND/OR A NUMBER** for each answer.*

In the problem-solving tests, students had to work in groups of four people and
26 .... to solve a problem. As they discussed the problem, **27** .... watched them. As well
as assessing the ability to speak, the problem-solving tested if people can **28** .... , organize their
thoughts and demonstrate they can be part of a **29** .... Re-sits of the final exams are held in
September. After that any problems are dealt with by **30** ....

Stop the recording when you hear 'That is the end of Section 3.'
Now check your answers to Section 3 of the test.

Section 4   Questions 31–40

Questions 31–33

Choose the correct letter A, B or C.

31 The Indian Ocean differs from the Atlantic and Pacific Oceans

    A by being closed in to the north.
    B by being warmer than both.
    C by extending into cold regions.

32 Approximately how much of the world's total ocean area does the Indian Ocean constitute?

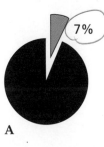
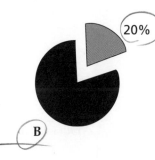
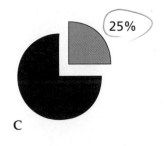

A   **B**   **C**

33 The island of Madagascar is

    A the tip of a submerged ridge.
    B the result of a volcanic eruption.
    C structurally part of the continent of Africa.

Questions 34 and 35

Complete the sentences below.

*Write **NO MORE THAN TWO WORDS** for each answer.*

34 Oceanographers and meteorologists are monitoring changes in the Indian ocean's temperature and ....

35 An assessment is being made of the impact of the changes on low-lying .... and ....

Questions 36–40

Complete the flow-chart below.

*Write **NO MORE THAN THREE WORDS** for each answer.*

Data Processing

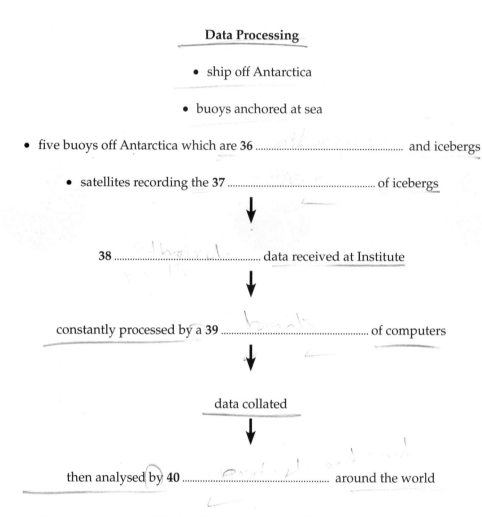

- ship off Antarctica

- buoys anchored at sea

- five buoys off Antarctica which are **36** .... and icebergs

- satellites recording the **37** .... of icebergs

↓

38 .... data received at Institute

↓

constantly processed by a **39** .... of computers

↓

data collated

↓

then analysed by **40** .... around the world

Stop the recording when you hear 'That is the end of Section 4'.
Before you check your answers to Section 4 of the test, go on to page 101.

Further practice for Listening Section 4

Questions 31–40

*Look at the following hints for **questions 31–40** and decide whether they are correct or not. Try to predict and answer the questions.*

31 something to do with a physical feature

....

32 something to do with size in relation to the rest of the world

....

33 something to do with what type of island it is.

....

34 something to do with a substance in the water

....

35 something to do with (the effect on) living things and where they live

....

36 something to do with what the buoys are doing or checking

....

37 something to do with a physical feature of icebergs

....

38 something to do with the nature of the data before they are processed

....

39 something to do with a series or group

....

40 something to do with types of machine

....

Now check your answers to these exercises. When you have done so, listen again to Section 4 of the test and decide whether you wish to change any of your answers. Then check your answers to Section 4 of the test.

Reading      Academic Reading   60 minutes

Reading Passage 1

*You should spend about 20 minutes on **Questions 1–13**, which are based on Reading Passage 1 below.*

English Heritage Blue Plaques Scheme 2

A   The blue plaques scheme has been running for over 140 years and is one of the oldest of its kind in the world. The idea of erecting 'memorial tablets' was first proposed by William Ewart MP in the House of Commons in 1863. It had an immediate impact on the public imagination, and in 1866 the Society of Arts (later Royal Society of Arts) founded an official plaques scheme. The Society erected its first plaque – to the poet Lord Byron – in 1867. In all, the Society of Arts erected 35 plaques; today, less than half of them survive, the earliest of which commemorates Napoleon III (1867). In 1901, the plaques scheme was taken over by London County Council (LCC), which erected nearly 250 plaques over the next 64 years and gave the scheme its popular appeal. It was under the LCC that the blue plaque design as we know it today was adopted, and the selection criteria were formalised. On the abolition of the LCC in 1965, the plaques scheme passed to the Greater London Council (GLC). The scheme changed little but the GLC was keen to broaden the range of people commemorated. The 262 plaques erected by the GLC include those to figures such as Sylvia Pankhurst, campaigner for women's rights; Samuel Coleridge-Taylor, composer of the Song of Hiawatha; and Mary Seacole, the Jamaican nurse and heroine of the Crimean War. Since 1986, English Heritage has managed the blue plaques scheme. So far, English Heritage has erected nearly 300 plaques, bringing the total number to over 800.

B   English Heritage receives about 100 suggestions for blue plaques each year, almost all of which come from members of the public. The background of each case is very different. Each nominated person has to meet basic selection criteria before they can be considered. Most importantly, they must have been dead for 20 years or have passed the centenary of their birth, whichever is the earlier. This delay allows a person's reputation to mature and ensures that their fame is long-lasting.

C   English Heritage's Blue Plaques Panel – representatives of various disciplines from across the country – considers all the suggestions which meet the basic criteria; on average, around 1 in 3 proposals are accepted. If a figure is rejected, proposers must wait a further 10 years before their suggestion can be considered again. Detailed research is carried out into the surviving addresses of shortlisted candidates, using sources such as autobiographies, electoral registers and post office directories.

D   As only one plaque is allowed per person, the house to be commemorated has to be chosen very carefully. Factors which are considered include length of residence and the accomplishments of a candidate during the relevant years. A significant place of work can also be considered.

E   Before a plaque can be erected, the owners and tenants of the building in question have to give their consent. Where listed buildings are involved, Listed Building Consent is sought from the relevant local authority. If such consents are granted, the plaque is designed, and then produced by a specialist manufacturer. It is normally ready within about two months. Plaques are set into the fabric of the building, flush with the wall face. The cost of plaque manufacture and installation are borne entirely by English Heritage. In all, it can take between 2 and 5 years from the initial suggestion to the erection of a plaque.

F   The exact form of the blue plaque, as we see it now, was a relatively late development, though certain guiding principles had been in place from the outset. The earliest plaques, erected in 1867, were blue. Their format, a circle with the name of the Society of Arts worked into a pattern around the edge, was used consistently by the Society over its 35 years of management.

G   Manufacture of each plaque is undertaken by the mixing and pouring of a thick clay slip into a casting mould. When sufficiently dry, the cast is removed and the outline of the inscription and border is piped onto the face of the plaque and filled with white glaze. Blue glaze is then applied to the background before firing. This process produces gently raised characters and border, a unique feature of English Heritage plaques. After firing, plaques usually have a thickness of 2 inches (50mm) and a final diameter of 19.5 inches (495mm), although smaller diameter plaques are sometimes used to meet special circumstances.

H   Plaques have been found to be extremely durable and have an almost indefinite life expectancy. Similar plaques erected by the Society of Arts have lasted, perfectly legible, for over one hundred years. Due to the slightly domed design, they are self-cleansing and require virtually no maintenance.

© Emily Cole, English Heritage

Questions 1–6

Reading Passage 1 has eight paragraphs **A–H**.

Which paragraph contains the following information?

*Write the correct letter, **A–H**, in boxes **1–6** on your answer sheet.*

> 1   the toughness of the plaques
>
> 2   the length of time it takes to produce a plaque
>
> 3   the way the Blue Plaques Panel functions
>
> 4   the conditions which need to be met in each case
>
> 5   the reasons behind selecting a house to be honoured
>
> 6   how the Blue Plaques scheme first started

Questions 7–10

Complete the diagram below.

*Choose **NO MORE THAN TWO WORDS AND/OR A NUMBER** from the passage for each answer.*

*Write your answers in boxes **7–10** on your answer sheet.*

A Blue Plaque

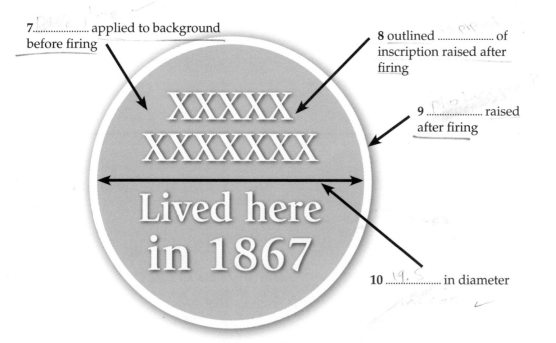

7 .... applied to background before firing

8 outlined .... of inscription raised after firing

9 .... raised after firing

10 .... in diameter

Questions 11–13

Do the following statements agree with the information in Reading Passage 1?

In boxes 11–13 on your answer sheet, write

TRUE   *if the statement agrees with the information*
FALSE   *if the statement contradicts the information*
NOT GIVEN   *if there is no information about the statement*

11   The GLC did not erect as many plaques as English Heritage has.

12   Rejected proposals are given a detailed explanation of their refusal.

13   The form of the blue plaque has not changed since it was first made.

Before you check your answers to Reading Passage 1, go on to page 106.

Further practice for Reading Passage 1

When you skim a passage to match sentences to paragraphs, it is important to recognise patterns or words that fit together. Often reading every word hides these patterns.

*Look at **Questions 1–6** and answer the following.*

Question 1

Do the following words relate to the toughness or the weakness of the blue plaque?

durable
to last
indefinite life expectancy

Question 2

Do the following words relate to the production or selection of a plaque?

designed
produce
ready within two months

Question 3

Do the following words relate to the way the Blue Plaques Panel works?

representatives
consider suggestions
criteria
research on suggestions

Question 4

Do the following words relate to marketing or the conditions for selection?

nominated
meet selection criteria
before
considered
must

Question 5

Do the following words relate to reasons for choosing a house or person to honour?

house
commemorate
choose
factors
considered

Question 6

Do the following words relate to the starting or the recent history of the Blue Plaques scheme?

has been running
140 years
oldest of its kind
first proposed 1866
founded
first plaque 1867

Now check your answers to these exercises. When you have done so, decide whether you wish to change any of your answers to Reading Passage 1. Then check your answers to Reading Passage 1.

Reading Passage 2

You should spend about 20 minutes on **Questions 14–27**, which are based on Reading Passage 2 on the following pages.

Questions 14–19

Reading Passage 2 has eight paragraphs **A–H**.

Choose the correct heading for paragraphs **B** and **D–H** from the list of headings below.

Write the correct number, **i–xi**, in boxes **14–19** on your answer sheet.

List of Headings
i   Testing acquired knowledge
ii   The way future performance is forecast through testing
iii   The Minnesota Multiphasic Personality Inventory
iv   Software tools in research explained
v   The use of a five-point scale in testing
vi   A test used to obtain a summary score of an individual's intelligence
vii   The method most widely used by psychologists in various situations
viii Subjective interests employed to predict future behaviour
ix   The different classes of standardized tests
x   The importance of prior learning in tests
xi   · Information gathered by self-reporting

Example	Answer
Paragraph A	**iv**

14 Paragraph B

Example	Answer
Paragraph C	**i**

15 Paragraph D

16 Paragraph E

17 Paragraph F

18 Paragraph G

19 Paragraph H

A   The software tools of research are typically more abundant than hardware tools in the social sciences. Software is usually thought of as meaning computer programs that tell the hardware what to do, but any tool not related to a physical device can be considered software. Included in this category are published tests and questionnaires.

B   Often researchers want to gather information related to a general area such as personality or intelligence. For these instances, the use of a standardized test may be the best choice. With already published tests you can be sure of both validity and reliability and can save a lot of time that might otherwise be spent on test construction. Standardized tests can be classified into five main categories: achievement, aptitude, interest, personality, and intelligence.

C   Achievement tests are designed specifically to measure an individual's previously learned knowledge or ability. They are available for many topic areas related to psychology, education, business, and other fields. Achievement tests require that prior learning take place and that this learning be demonstrated in order to pass.

D   Aptitude tests attempt to predict an individual's performance in some activity at some point in the future. They do not require any specific prior learning although basic knowledge related to reading and writing is usually required and some preparation, such as studying up on math formulas or sentence structure, can be helpful. A well-known example of this type is the Scholastic Achievement Test (SAT), designed to predict future college performance.

E   Interest inventories also require only general knowledge but no preparation is needed. These tests look at an individual's subjective interests in order to make predictions about some future behavior or activity. Perhaps the most used interest inventory is the Strong Interest Inventory, which compares interests related to specific careers in order to help guide an individual's career path. Endorsed interests are compared with the interests of successful individuals in various fields and predictions are made regarding the test-taker's fit with the various career fields.

F   Typically designed to assess and diagnose personality and mental health related disorders, personality tests are used extensively by psychologists in clinical, educational, and business related settings. By far the most widely used test of this type is the Minnesota Multiphasic Personality Inventory, Second Edition (MMPI-2), which compares an individual's responses on a series of true-false items to those suffering from various mental disorders such as depression, schizophrenia, and anxiety. The theory behind the test argues that if you endorse items similar to the items endorsed by those with depression, for example, then the chances that you are also depressed increases.

G   Intelligence tests could be classified as aptitude tests since they are sometimes used to predict future performance. They could also be classified as personality tests since they can be used to diagnose disorders such as learning disabilities and mental retardation. However, because of their limited scope, we will place them in their own category. The purpose of an intelligence test is to attain a summary score or intelligence quotient (IQ) of an individual's intellectual ability. Scores are compared to each other and can be broken down into different subcategories depending on the intelligence test used. The most commonly used tests of this type are the Wechsler Scales, including the Wechsler Adult Intelligence Scale (WAIS), the Wechsler Intelligence Scale for Children (WISC), and the Wechsler Preschool and Primary Scale of Intelligence (WPPSI).

H   Self-response questionnaires are a great way to gather large amounts of information in a relatively short amount of time. A questionnaire, similar to a survey you might see on a web page, allows subjects to respond to questions, rate responses, or offer opinions. Their responses can then be used to place them in specific categories or groups or can be compared to other subjects for data analysis. A concern with self-report, however, is the accuracy of the responses. Unlike direct observation, there is no way of knowing if the subject has told the truth or whether or not the question was understood as intended. There are several different methods for gathering information on a questionnaire or survey, including a Likert scale, the Thurstone technique, and the semantic differential. The Likert scale is a popular method used in surveys because it allows the researcher to quantify opinion based items. Questions are typically grouped together and rated or responded to based on a five-point scale. This scale typically ranges in order from one extreme to the other, such as (1) very interested; (2) somewhat interested; (3) unsure; (4) not very interested; and (5) not interested at all. Items that might be rated with this scale representing the subject's level of interest could include a list of careers or academic majors, for example.

Questions 20–23

Choose the correct letter A, B, C or D.

Write your answers in boxes 20–23 on your answer sheet.

20 Tests that are already on the market

   A need some form of reconstruction.
   B fail to ensure validity and reliability.
   C guarantee validity and reliability.
   D waste large amounts of time.

21 Some knowledge of reading and writing

   A is commonly not necessary in aptitude tests.
   B is normally a requirement in aptitude tests.
   C is less important in aptitude tests than other tests.
   D is as important as prior learning in aptitude tests.

22 With interest inventories, subjective interests are examined to

   A test people's general knowledge.
   B help people change their career.
   C compare individual's backgrounds.
   D forecast future behaviour or activity.

23 Intelligence tests could come under aptitude tests

   A because they can be used to forecast future performance.
   B since they are not used very widely.
   C as they can be broken down into different sub-groups.
   D because they are sometimes used to diagnose learning disabilities.

Questions 24–26

Do the following statements agree with the claims of the writer in Reading Passage 2?

In boxes 24–26 on your answer sheet, write

YES   *if the statement reflects the claims of the writer*
NO   *if the statement contradicts the claims of the writer*
NOT GIVEN   *if it is impossible to say what the writer thinks of this*

24 The Wechsler Scales are the only type of intelligence test now used.

25 Where large quantities of data need to be collected fairly quickly self-response questionnaires work well.

26 The Likert Scale ensures greater accuracy than other techniques.

Question 27

Choose the correct letter A, B, C or D.

Write your answer in box 27 on your answer sheet.

27 Which of the following is the most suitable heading for Reading Passage 2?

   A Different types of intelligence test
   B How personality can be tested
   C The importance of aptitude tests
   D The various software tools of research

Before you check your answers to Reading Passage 2, go on to page 111.

Further practice for Reading Passage 2

Paragraph headings

In questions with paragraph headings, it is important to understand how to interpret the headings themselves.

Question 14

*Look at paragraph heading **ix**.*

Which of the following are synonyms of the word *classes*?

> stages
> categories
> types
> kinds

....

Question 15

*Look at paragraph heading **ii**.*

1 Which words are synonyms of the word *way*?

> method
> how ...
> cause
> means

....

2 Which words are synonyms of the word *forecast*?

> predict
> assume
> project
> anticipate
> estimate

....

Question 16

*Look at paragraph heading **viii**.*

What nouns can you make from the verbs in **15.2** above?

....

....

....

....

....

....

Question 17

*Look at paragraph heading **vii**.*

Which words are related to the word *method*?

> means
> technique
> test
> examination
> theory

....

Question 18

*Look at paragraph heading **vi**.*

Is it possible to give a synonym for the word *intelligence*?

....

Question 19

*Look at paragraph heading **xi**.*

Is it possible to give a synonym for the word *self-reporting*?

....

Now check your answers to these exercises. When you have done so, decide whether you wish to change any of your answers to Reading Passage 2. Then check your answers to Reading Passage 2.

Reading Passage 3

*You should spend about 20 minutes on **Questions 28–40**, which are based on Reading Passage 3 below.*

Much ado about almost nothing

The public outcry over genetically modified foods offers several lessons for those working and investing in nanotechnology.

1 *"THE time for discussion of the rights and wrongs of GM crops has passed. Intense and consistent economic sabotage and intimidation are what will make the commercialisation of GM crops an unattractive option."*

2 Words like these, from an article in the current edition of *Earth First!*, a radical environmental journal, send shivers down the spines of those involved in commercialising biotechnology. The strength of public disapproval of genetically modified organisms (GMOs) was a shock and a surprise to most of those involved. Now, some people are wondering whether nanotechnology – a term that covers the manipulation of matter at scales of a millionth of a millimetre – could be in for similar treatment and, if so, whether there are lessons that its protagonists can learn from the public backlash against biotechnology.

Profit of doom

3 In a neglected corner, amid thousands of participants at a Nanotech conference held in Boston last week, Jeffrey Matsuura, a law professor at the University of Dayton, in Ohio, stood next to his unprepossessing poster of his work. His warning, however, was pertinent to everyone there – especially the investors who were scouring the conference for opportunities. And this is that several of the factors that created a public backlash against biotechnology are already at work within nanotechnology. Dr Matsuura says that biotechnologists assumed that the public would quickly recognise and appreciate biotech's potential for improving the quality of life. Instead, the risks captured the attention of the media and much of the general public. Well-fed European consumers met the suggestion of cheaper food, in particular, with scepticism. Many felt that the gains would accrue to the companies which had developed GMOs, while the risks of growing and consuming the crops would be taken on by the public.

4 Dr Matsuura believes that public perception of nanotechnology is developing along a similar track. Like those of biotechnology, the first applications of nanotechnology will bring little obvious benefit to consumers. Better, cheaper materials, and hidden manufacturing efficiencies that benefit producers first, are redolent of the 'advantages' of biotech – namely reduced applications of agricultural chemicals, which help to keep the cost down while raising yields. Obvious consumer benefits, such as improvements in medicine, are further away.

5 This should not matter – consumers do benefit eventually, even from cost savings. And yet, in alliance with a feeling that there are hazards involved, an absence of immediate benefits could turn public opinion against nanotech quite rapidly. And potential hazards there are. Concerns over out-of-control, self-replicating 'nanobots' that would eventually consume and transform the entire planet into a 'grey goo' are absurd. And yet, it is true that novel 'nanoparticles' might have real toxicological risks.

6 Nanoparticles are so small that, if inhaled, they could become lodged in the lungs. In theory, they are small enough to enter living cells and accumulate there. And in January Ken Donaldson, a professor of respiratory toxicology at the University of Edinburgh, told a Royal Institution seminar in London that, once inhaled, ultrafine carbon particles can move to the brain and blood.

7 There are already several products that use nanoparticles already on the market, such as sunscreen and car parts. Though all this may sound alarming, people are already exposed to nanoparticles of many different kinds, and have been throughout history. Soot, for example, is composed of carbon

nanoparticles. Nevertheless, nanoparticles from sources such as diesel soot, welding fumes and photocopier toner are already associated with ill-health. The prospect of more such particles is likely to worry many. No wonder that several people at the conference in Boston mentioned the need to address public fears over nanotechnology "aggressively".

8 One of these was Clayton Teague, the director of America's National Nanotechnology Co-ordination Office. He says the American government is as sensitive to any indication of true health risk as any member of the public. Several large and well-funded studies on the environmental and health risks of nanotechnology are now under way.

9 Dr Teague adds that any decisions about nanotechnology will be made carefully and based on solid scientific data. But even if science gives the

go-ahead, another one of Dr Matsuura's lessons is that this might not necessarily win the day, and that fear over potential abuses and accidents may dominate the debate.

10 One piece of advice Dr Matsuura gives is that everyone involved should have a consistent message. If investors are told a technology will change the world, someone who is concerned about the risks cannot then be told that the same technology is no big deal. It strikes a false note to say that something can be both revolutionary and nothing to worry about, he says. Such inconsistencies will breed public mistrust and fear.

Product placement

11 Donald Reed is a senior consultant with Ecos, a business-advisory firm based in Sydney, Australia, that acts as an intermediary between corporations and activists. Mr Reed goes as far as to recommend that companies think about the early products they choose to pursue – in particular, whether they can demonstrate the "societal value" of these products. For example, it might be worth emphasising that one of the early products of nanotechnology could be cheap and efficient photovoltaic materials, which are used to generate electricity from sunlight.

Questions 28–31

Look at the following people and the list of statements below.

Match each person with the correct statement.

Write the correct letter, A–G, in boxes 28–31 on your answer sheet.

28 Clayton Teague

29 Ken Donaldson

30 Donald Reed

31 Jeffrey Matsuura

List of Statements

A   Nanotechnology is being affected by factors that created opposition to biotechnology.

B   Europeans have the most to gain from nantotechnology development.

C   Sound scientific data will be the basis of any decisions about nanotechnology.

D   Governments cannot shape the development of nanotechnology.

E   Nanotechology is not a cause for concern.

F   Carbon nanoparticles can be breathed in and then move to the brain and blood.

G   Companies should show how their early nanotechnology products can benefit society.

Questions 32–35

Complete the sentences.

*Choose **NO MORE THAN THREE WORDS** from the passage for each answer.*

Write your answers in boxes 32–35 on your answer sheet.

32 Strong public disapproval of .... came as a shock to those working in the area.

33 Europeans reacted to the suggestion of cheaper food with ....

34 Anxiety about 'nanobots' that would in time change the planet is ....

35 Nanoparticles from photocopier toner are already linked to ....

Questions 36–40

Complete the summary using the list of words A–L below.

Write your answers in boxes 36–40 on your answer sheet.

Some people believe that nanotechnology could face a **36** .... fate to biotechnology. Rather than welcoming the **37** ...., the media and much of the general public focused their attention on the **38** .... of biotechnology. So it is important to emphasize the immediate **39** .... of nanotechnology; otherwise, the public could adopt a negative **40** .... towards nanotech. It is therefore important for everyone involved to be consistent.

A	worse	D	particles	G	dangers	J	former
B	greater	E	costs	H	thoughts	K	attitude
C	devices	F	latter	I	advantages	L	comparable

Writing  Academic Writing 60 minutes

WRITING TASK 1

You should spend about 20 minutes on this task.

> The bar chart below shows the employment of all male and female workers by occupation in the UK in the year 2005.

> Summarize the information by selecting and reporting the main features, and make comparisons where relevant.

Write at least 150 words.

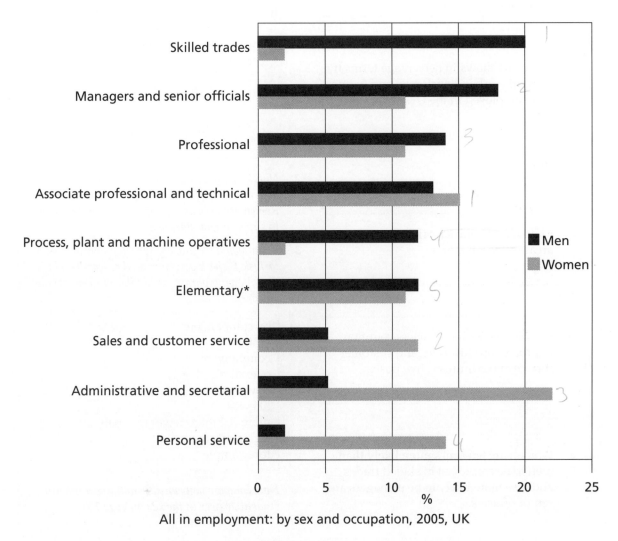

All in employment: by sex and occupation, 2005, UK

* elementary occupations = labourers and catering assistants

Before you write your answer to Task 1, go on to page 116.

Further practice for Writing Task 1

Always remember to write in paragraphs and to summarize the data and then prove your summary with examples.

1 *Are the statements below True about the bar chart? If they are not, correct them. There may be more than one possible answer.*

a Generally speaking, women tend to be more involved in managerial jobs like skilled trades, senior officials and professional occupations.

....

....

....

b The chart shows in percentage terms the areas of work in which men and women were employed in the UK in the year 2005.

....

....

....

c Males and females work in very similar areas of the job market.

....

....

d By contrast, women are less common in professions like sales and customer service and administrative posts.

....

....

e Women are ten times more likely than men to be employed in skilled trades and also more likely to be managers and senior officials.

....

....

....

f Similar proportions of men and women work in elementary occupations such as labourers and catering assistants.

....

....

g For every seven female employees in personal services there was one male.

....

....

h For example, 20 per cent of the workforce involved in skilled trades were male, while only 2 per cent were female.

....

....

....

2 *Now write your own answer for Task 1. You may use some of the sentences or phrases above. Remember to insert specific data from the chart to support your statements.*

3 *When you have finished writing your answer to Task 1, check you have used at least half of the following phrases or similar phrases in your answer:*

> by comparison
> while
> compared to
> overall
> however
> likewise
> more (...) than/fewer (...) than
> a greater proportion
> for example

Now compare your answer with the authentic student answer in the key on page 151.

WRITING TASK 2

You should spend about 40 minutes on this task.

Write about the following topic:

> *With recent developments in technology like e-books, some people feel that printed media like books, newspapers, and magazines will soon be a thing of the past. Others feel that these forms of media will never disappear.*
>
> *What is your opinion?*

Give reasons for your answer and include any relevant examples from your own knowledge or experience.

Write at least 250 words.

Before you write your answer to Task 2, go on to page 118.

Further practice for Writing Task 2

As you write your answer, ask yourself a question after every sentence. It can help you write an appropriate answer.

1   *Answer the questions below to create Paragraph 1.*

    a What do some people feel about the advances like electronic books?

    ....

    ....

    ....

    b By contrast, what do other people believe about the future of media such as books?

    ....

    ....

    ....

    c And what do you personally think about current developments?

    ....

    ....

    ....

2   *Answer the questions below to create*

    c However, if they had only a lifeless piece of electronic equipment or a screen on a computer to look at, how would they feel?

    ....

    ....

    d Moreover, what other example can you give about the way books and magazines look compared to information on a screen, even a flat portable screen?

    ....

    ....

    e What is the result of this?

    ....

    ....

    f However, with more and more newspapers and some books on line, is it possible to stop e-books entering our lives?

    ....

    ....

Now write similar questions to help you write a paragraph on e-books and give your opinion.

....

....

....

....

....

....

....

....

When you have finished, compare your answer with the authentic student answer in the key on page 151.

Speaking  11–14 minutes

PART 1 Introduction and interview (4–5 minutes)

In this part of the examination you will be asked questions about yourself and familiar topics.

EXAMPLE

Bicycles
- What is your name?
- Where do you come from?
- Tell me about the use of bicycles in your country.
- How popular are bicycles in your country?
- Are they used more now than in the past? Why? Why not?
- What do bicycles mean to you?

PART 2 Individual long turn (3–4 minutes)

Describe a well-known person from the world of sport (or films) that you would like to meet.

You should say:

who this person is
what this person has done
why this person is well-known

and explain why you would like to meet this person.

You will have to talk about this topic for one to two minutes. You have one minute to think about what you are going to say. You can make some notes to help you if you wish.

Now look at the Further Practice section on page 120.

Now look at the Further Practice section on page 120.

PART 3 Two-way discussion (4–5 minutes)

In this part of the exam, the examiner will discuss a topic with you. The topic is usually related in some way to the topic in Part 2, but the questions will be of a more abstract nature.

Role models in the sports world

Example questions:

Do sportsmen and women make good role models for young people? Why? Why not?
Are we too concerned with the sports stars rather than the sports themselves?
Why do you think sports stars are paid so much? Is this justified? Why? Why not?

Job changes

Example questions:

Do you think people are happy to stay in the same job for a long time these days?
What types of jobs are popular these days? Why?
Which jobs do you think will be popular in the future? Why?

Now look at the Further Practice section on page 121.

Further practice for Speaking

PART 2

Try to be natural when you speak. React to what the examiner gives you rather than just speaking from memory. However, use phrases to help you organize your answer.

1   For **Part 2** *on page 119, write short notes of one or two words for each statement below.*

    a   If I were able to choose anyone I would like to meet, it would have to be

    ....

    ....

    b   She/He has made a big contribution to the world of sport

    ....

    ....

    c   She/He has influenced young people

    ....

    ....

    d   She/He has ... and

    ....

    ....

    e   Moreover/What's more/Besides this/Also/In addition to this, she/he has

    ....

    ....

    f   What has made her/him famous is

    ....

    ....

    g   She/he is

    ....

    ....

2   *Develop your notes in* **1** *by using:*

by	because	through	which
and so			

adjectives:
*inspiring   inspirational
talented   likeable   motivating
friendly   interesting   nice*

verbs:
*improve   make   help
encourage   foster   promote
spread   advance*

3   *Now practise answering Part 2 with a partner.*

PART 3

Developing your answer in the third part of the speaking is very important.

1 *Decide which questions in Part 3 each student answer 1–3 below matches.*

> **Student 1**: I think that people are less likely to stay in the same job these days, because **1** .... and even from country to country in search of a good job. For example, you now see large numbers of people from all over Europe searching for work, as **2** .... This is not just in low-paid work like catering, but in well-paid work in the business and financial world.

> **Student 2**: I think sportsmen and women are a good influence on young people, because **3** .... And so young people will aspire to achieve what these people have attained in sport or other fields, as **4** ...., which is beneficial for the individual and the community at large. For example, for many young men or women, the aim is **5** ...., whether as a top athlete or in another field.

> **Student 3**: Sometimes, however, sports stars can be a negative influence on the young. If a footballer, for example, does something wrong during a game, like kicking or hitting someone, **6** .... What makes it bad is that **7** .... As a result, **8** ....

2 *Add reasons a–h in a suitable place 1–8 in the student answers in the first column.*

a they can act as role-models that young people can emulate or look up to

b to be like someone that they admire and attain what they have done

c they think that their behaviour, good or bad, is acceptable

d successful people tend to inspire other people to succeed

e it is much easier for them to move from job to job

f their friends have done the same and found good jobs

g young people are impressionable and hero worship such people whatever they do

h this is reported in the news and is then seen by fans

3 *Practise asking and answering the questions in Part 3 with a partner. Remember to develop your answer with reasons, results and purposes.*

Use these expressions to show your opinion:

> In my opinion
> I think
> I believe
> From my point of view
> I personally feel
> What I personally think is that …
> I consider
>
> positive adjectives:
> *useful   helpful   important*
> *inspiring   inspirational*
> *talented   motivating*
>
> negative expressions:
> *cause trouble/problems*
> *be a nuisance*
> *dangerous*

Key and Explanation

TEST ONE

p8–14 Listening

Further practice and guidance (p11–12)

Personal details

1   Can/Could you give me/Can I take/ have/What's/your name (please)?

2   And (can you give me/can I take/have/ what's) your telephone/mobile number?

3   How many nights/How long are you going to stay/do you plan to stay? Can you tell me how many nights/how long you are going to/plan to stay?

4   And what type/grade of hotel would you like/are you looking for?/ Can you tell me what type/grade of hotel you are looking for/you would like …?

Completing sentences

1   7   return date

    8   save

    9   additional charge

    10 cancellation

2   no

3   7   Can/Could you tell me when you'd like to go away/leave?

    8   How much is the holiday/does the holiday cost (excluding insurance)?

    9   What reductions/discounts/offers do you have at the moment?

    10 I'll just give you your/a reservation/ booking reference (number).

Gap-filling

11 a noun (related to time)

12 a noun (possibly with an adjective or a compound noun)

13 a noun (in the plural)

Understanding plans

15 is left of the entrance/in the bottom left-hand corner of the plan.

16 is in the centre of the plan.

17 is in the top right-hand corner/beside the sports area.

18 is in the top left-hand corner of the plan.

19 is above the flats in the bottom left-hand corner of the plan.

20 is near the workshops in the bottom right-hand corner of the plan.

p8–9 Listening Section 1

Questions 1–4

1   Framlington

2   44 11 92

3   5/five nights (only)

4   4/four

Questions 5 and 6

B and C: in any order. John asks: *What's the hotel like?* The Receptionist describes it. Then John says: *what appeals to me most … hotel's very convenient for all the water buses. And …a terrace with the room I really find very appealing. These are big plusses!* The other items are not given.

Questions 7–10

7   **17th March**: The receptionist says: *Can you tell me when you'd like to leave?* Note that *depart* and *leave* are related.

8   **716**: Listen for a question related to cost.

9   **15/fifteen**: The receptionist says: *… you get a further 15% reduction …*

10 **FAPSJM15**: The receptionist says: *I'll just give you a reference for the reservation.*

p10 Listening Section 2

Questions 11–13

11 **decade**: Listen for the word *development* and *lying unused for ...*

12 **(small) business park**: Listen for *pressure* and *training* to prepare for the answer.

13 **(local) organizations/organisations**: The sentence helps you predict the type of word. It is some kind of group. Note the noun is in the plural. The word *sponsorship* helps you listen for the answer.

Questions 14–20

14 **Parkside**: Follow the instructions. The street is at the bottom.

15 **40 studio flats**: The block of flats is: *on the left of the entrance, in the bottom left-hand corner of the plan.*

16 **ornamental lake**: The word to listen for is *centre*.

17 **swimming pool**: Listen for: *... the top right-hand corner...; Just here beside the pitches ...*

18 **(flower) garden**: Listen for: *.... in the top left-hand corner.*

19 **play area**: Listen for: *In the bottom left corner* and *above the block of flats.*

20 **café**: Listen for: *bottom right-hand corner of the park.*

p13 Listening Section 3

Questions 21–23

21 **C**: The Registrar Andy Matthews asks: *Have you any problems with the course itself?* Rosana replies: *I think the course is really worthwhile* (valuable). She does not mention speed (B) and *worthless* (A) is the opposite of *worthwhile*.

22 **B**: The Wednesday sessions make her: *... too exhausted for my work on Thursdays and Fridays.* Even though she may arrive home late on Wednesday, she doesn't give this as a reason. She likes the course tutors, so C is not correct.

23 **A**: Andy says: *... but you realise it's possible you'll have a different tutor.* Neither B nor C are mentioned.

Questions 24 and 25

D and E in any order. Listen for positive words about the new programme. Rosana says: *It's the flexibility ... that is very useful. And what makes it even more interesting is that I don't have to spend a lot of time travelling to and from the university on the Wednesday.* The other alternatives are not mentioned.

Questions 26–30

26 **course diary**: Andy says: *... expected to keep a written course diary.*

27 **written exam**: Andy says: *... a written exam ... will account for 30 per cent.* The information is the other way round, so you need to be careful.

28 **design**: Listen for the word *course work*. Andy then says: *The design portfolio, which you need to present at the end ...*

29 **50 per cent/percent/%**: This comes closely after the previous one, so be careful.

30 **fashion show**: Listen for the word *present*.

p13 Listening Section 4

Questions 31–37

31 **A**: The student says that the collection of the data was: *... to find out what effect, if any, various buildings have on people's mood.* So the survey is not about collecting data about buildings themselves (B), nor the attractiveness of buildings (C).

32 **C**: Listen for the word *originally*. The reason given by the student is related to time. The student says : *... were worried that doing the questionnaire would be too time-consuming for people to fill in, so we gave up the idea.* It is not about the time taken to produce (A) nor the difficulty of writing the questions (B).

33 **B**: Listen for *scale* and *using the scale*. The result of using the scale was the fact that the information was easier to collect. The student says: *... meant that it would be much simpler to record people's reactions.*

34 **C**: Listen for the word *images*: The reason given was to do with colour: *... we used colour rather than black and white to make the detail on the images clearer.*

35 A: Listen for a word related to *preserve*: *protection*.

36 A: Listen for: *We also asked a sample of the general public including ...* B and C are not mentioned although the word *exited* is mentioned in relation to *tourists*.

37 B: *We found that we had to appoint a leader to stop us pulling in different directions.* There is no mention of A or C.

Questions 38–40

38 A

39 C

40 D

p15–29 Academic Reading

Further practice and guidance (p19–20)

Title

1   yes

2   yes

3   Yes.
     Cause: *As populations grow ...*
     Effect: *people have to look for ...*

Section A and example

1   yes

2   yes

3   no

4   yes

Question 1

1   yes

2   yes

3   no

Question 2

1   no

2   no

3   yes

Question 3

1   yes

2   yes

3   yes

Question 4

1   no

2   yes

3   yes

4   yes

p15–18 Reading Passage 1

Questions 1–4

1   (iii):   The answer is in the first line of the section: *impact*. Look at the heading for the word that shows you the organization of the section: *effects*. Then look at the type of effects: *population growth*. This is connected with the problem in section A: *expansion of the human population*. The relationship is cause and effect. Look for other effect words: *impact, ensure, fuelling, turned into, becomes*. Also notice the words *Urbanization is now; more evident than previously; drift from; springing up*. These and other words indicate change. Heading vi is not possible, as there is no description.

2   (i):   The section contains solutions up to the present time (*hitherto; has been; most common practice; build upwards; build downwards*) to the effects described in the previous section. You can recognise the solution heading as it begins with *how*. Heading iv is only an example, which could be removed without affecting the meaning of the section.

3 (ii): Look at the heading for the word that shows you the organization of the section: *predictions … future solutions*. The word *theories* in the second sentence is associated with the word *predictions*. The dates give you a clear link with the heading. Note the connection between this section and the last: *past/future solutions*.

4 (vii): Look at the words: *… no longer just a dream, but a reality* in the first sentence; *… planned for the near future*; *… are not fanciful*. They give the writer's belief. Heading viii is not possible, because without the example the section still has its original meaning.

Questions 5–8

5 worldwide phenomenon. The answer can be found in Section B which deals with people moving to cities: *urbanization*.

6 valuable resource. Scan for a word which is related to demand: *hungry*. Look for the result of the urbanization, in the last line of the first paragraph of Section B.

7 agricultural technology. Note the word limit, so you cannot write *developments in*; also note the synonym, *changes*, in the question. The answer is in the first line of the second paragraph of Section B. Use the words *feed/human race* to help you scan. Note the relationship between *be guaranteed* and *ensure*.

8 infrastructure facilities. Scan for the word *accommodation*. It is in the middle of the third sentence of the same paragraph. Note: *the various/range of … .*

Questions 9–13

9 Yes. The answer is at the end of paragraph 2 in Section B. Note the statement says that there is a link, but not what the link is. You have to check whether the two pieces of information are linked. In the text the link is one of cause and effect.

10 Yes. Look at heading iv: the example of building underground. Scan for *underground building*: the end of the first paragraph, Section C. The question is a cause and effect statement: see *led to*.

11 Not Given. Scan for *Japan* and *Dubai*. You have two pieces of information: the airport and the housing complex. You have to check if the cost is compared. However, there is no comparison of cost, so you do not know the answer.

12 No. Look at Section D. Other people predict the future habitation of the solar system. So Arthur C Clarke is not the only one. Note the connection with heading ii. The word *only* is common in this type of question. When you see the word *only* always check if there are other people etc. involved.

13 No. The answer is in Section E. As you know the questions are in order, then you can expect the answer somewhere after number 12. Scan for *habitation in outer space*; the first line. The word *unimaginable* is the opposite of the meaning in the text. Look at the words: *no longer just a dream, but a reality; are not far-off; I am sure I am not alone in fantasizing*. See the answer for 4 above. When you see an obvious positive or negative adjective, verb, noun etc. in the question, check the reading passage for their synonyms or opposites.

Further practice and guidance (p25–26)

Question 22

1 no

2 yes

3 yes

4 yes

Question 23

1 yes

2 no

3 yes

Question 24

1 yes

2 yes

3 yes

4 no

Question 25
1   yes
2   yes
3   yes
4   no
Question 26
1   yes
2   yes
3   yes
Question 27
1   yes
2   yes

p21–24 Reading Passage 2

Questions 14–16

B, E, F in any order. As the word *salt* is in every statement, use other words to scan. Start with the names: *Kansas* etc. B is in paragraph 6 – look for the words *French Revolution*; E is in paragraph 2 – *some 14,000 commercial applications*. Note that the applications are not countless. The answer for F is in paragraph 1.

Questions 17–21

17 **essential element**: The answer is in the first line of paragraph 2. You know the answer begins with a vowel; see the word *an* in the summary. This also tells you the answer is a noun/noun adjective and in the singular.

18 **applications**: See 14–16. Remember what you have seen in other questions. Scan for the *thousands* or *000* in paragraph 2; Note the words *business/commercial*.

19 **portable commodity**: Scan for the word *economies*; the second line of paragraph 4. Note the words *prized/precious*.

20 **taxes**: The answer is in the second line of paragraph 5.

21 **spirits**: Scan for the word *evil*. See the last line of paragraph 8. Note that *malevolent* means *evil*.

Questions 22–27

22 **True**: See paragraph 4: *researcher M.R. Bloch conjectured ...* The word *conjectured* shows Bloch is not sure: *It has been suggested*. If you remove *it has been suggested that* the answer becomes *Not Given*.

23 **Not Given**. See paragraph 5. We know that the Chinese Emperor imposed one of the first known taxes and it was on salt. We do not know if there were other salt taxes that were not known about.

24 **False**: The answer is in paragraph 5: *to this day*. Find the name *Ethiopia*. Note that if you remove the words *no longer* the statement is then *True*.

25 **False**: Scan for *Erie Canal*. The answer is in the seventh paragraph. The information is given: *half*. This contradicts *most*.

26 **True**: Scan for the word *Hopi*. It is in paragraph 9. Look for a word connected with penalize: *punished*. The statement gives you the reason for placing salt deposits far away.

27 **True**: Look at the last paragraph. Notice the word *connected*.

p27–29 Reading Passage 3

Questions 28–33

28 **I**:   You scan for information that is presented as negative.

29 **D**: Scan for words that relate to impact: *effect*. Remember the structure 'cause– effect– solution'. In this particular passage, you can expect *effect* to come after volunteering has been described. The word *individual* also helps you to scan.

30 **G**: Scan for *requirement* or a synonym: *prerequisites*; *selflessness* and *self-interest*. Even if you do not know the word *prerequisites*, you can scan for a paragraph which contains personal qualities.

31 **C**: You scan for the type of volunteer work that people do. You can predict that in many cases this will be somewhere at the beginning rather than the end. Scan for nouns like *sectors, activities, fields*; verbs like *involved, worked in, participated in*; names of different fields like *community, international/ foreign* etc.

32 **E**: The key scan words here are *benefit* and *young*.

33 A: Scan for an opinion about volunteering. You can predict this is at the beginning, because the writer is saying what people wrongly believe about volunteering. Then he says what it is.

Questions 34–37

34 D: The answer is in paragraph A. The abbreviation helps you find the answer. It is towards the beginning, because the questions are in order. The survey was about which people participated/were involved in volunteering. It was not about why (A); nor about how many (B); nor about how many rich people (C). The results, however, revealed that rich people tend to volunteer more, but that was a *result* of the survey, not the reason for doing it.

35 B: The answer is in paragraph B. Scan for the phrase *qualifications*: *Among people with a degree or postgraduate qualification, 79 per cent had volunteered informally and 57 per cent had volunteered formally in the previous 12 months; For people with no qualifications the corresponding proportions were 52 per cent and 23 per cent*. So A and C contradict the answer. D is incorrect, because qualified people are not the only ones.

36 C: The previous question helps you find the answer. Scan for *rich people, goals, children, time* and *guilt* or their synonyms. The reason comes at the end of paragraph B after the results of the survey have been revealed.The writer uses a question to suggest the relationship between time and money. No information about the other three alternatives is given.

37 A: Scan for *benefit to people* in general. Note the link between volunteers, situations and systems. This comes in paragraph D before the more specific benefit to young people in paragraph E.

Questions 38–40

38 E: Ask yourself: What ability of being a volunteer is required? The word *requirements* helps you find the paragraph (See question 30 above and paragraph G). Look at the sentence endings A–F. The only one dealing with a quality is E.

39 C: Ask yourself: What can the unemployed use volunteering as? Scan for *unemployed* and *use of volunteering as a way/means* etc. Find the word *stepping-stone* in paragraph H. You can match *unemployed* with *work/ job/employment*.

40 A: Ask yourself: What do employers tend to do? Scan for the word *employers*. The answer is in paragraph F: *... generally look favourably on people; ... to satisfy employers' demands ...*

p30–34 Academic Writing

Further practice and guidance (p31–33)

Task 1

Language to describe movements in graphs

1
to plunge	I
to soar	D
to rise (gradually)	H
to fluctuate	E
to hit a peak	G
to dip	F
to bottom out	C
to remain flat	B

2
a   fluctuated
b   rise/fall
c   hit
d   rise
e   dipped/fell/plunged
f   bottomed
g   plunged/fell

3
decline: fall, dip
plummet: plunge
increase: rise, soar
reach a high: hit/reach a peak
rocket: soar
decrease: fall, dip
jump: soar, rise
level off: bottom out

4 **a** It is noticeable that *the numbers for the London Underground* match and at times exceed the national figures.

b Generally speaking, all three networks *show an upward trend*.

c By 2004/05, the National rail network *had reached a high of around 1.1 billion* passenger journeys.

d Moreover, journey numbers for the London Underground showed a similar pattern *falling from approximately 700 million to about 500 million*.

e The graph illustrates passenger journeys on *three railway systems in Great Britain* between 1950 and 2005.

f Both systems exceeded the billion passenger journey mark, with the 1980s and the early 2000s *witnessing the most noticeable increases*.

g The light railway and metro systems *did not have as many passenger journeys as* the other two networks.

h The most striking characteristic is that the journey numbers for the National rail network *correspond to those for the London Underground*.

5 **i** summarizing sentences   b

ii comparisons   a, d, f, g, h

iii an introduction   e

iv striking features   a, h

7 **a** **yes**. It contains 188 words. In the exam you must not write below 150 words.

b **yes**. It is necessary to have paragraphs. Apart from in the introduction or conclusion, avoid paragraphs of one sentence only.

c **yes**. An attempt has been made to change some of the words (*shows/ provides information; journeys/trips*) and grammar structure (*the number of passenger railway journeys made/how many trips were made by passengers in three railway systems*)

d **yes**. It has an overview: It is clear that the trends for all three networks are upward with the most striking feature being the similarity between the National rail network and the London underground. Always make sure that you have a summarizing statement.

The main features have been selected: the similarity between the National rail network and the London Underground; *London Underground experienced a similar, but less pronounced, decline; both followed a very similar pattern; light railway and metro systems carried fewer passengers than the other two networks.*

There are comparisons: in the overview at the end; in the third sentence beginning *Likewise*; in the sentence beginning with *Thereafter*; and in the first sentence of the third paragraph, beginning *By comparison*.

e **no**. A conclusion could be added, but the overview is sufficient.

f **yes**. Note the range of verbs: *fell; experienced ... decline; followed a very similar pattern; climbed; seeing the sharpest increases; carried; picked up, reaching*. Different nouns are used (*systems/networks*); nouns instead of verbs (*decline/increases*); different verb forms (*picked up, reaching*). There is variety in the language.

g **no**.

Task 1   Authentic Student Answer

The graph shows the number of commuters using London Underground, the national rail network and the light rail and metro systems in Great Britain from 1950 to 2004/5.

Overall, the number of passenger journeys made on the three systems increased, but on London Underground it increased dramaticly. The most striking figure was that one billon journeys were made a year on the national rail network in the 1950s. At that time, the London Underground was carrying around 750 million passengers and they fell to 500 million in 1980 compared to 600 million on the national rail network.

From the beginning of the 1980s, the number of passenger journeys on all three main ways of transport rose rappidly. The number of passenger journeys on London Underground and the national rail network were very similar throughout the remaining period, rising to approximately 1.1 billion in 2004/05.

The period ended with the national railway slightly up than the starting point and London Underground at the second place of just under one billon and light and metro at third place with approximatly 200 million passenger journeys.

Word count: 182

Grade: 7

The key points are covered, and are well organized into paragraphs and highlighted clearly, despite some lapses in the second paragraph. Cohesive devices are fairly well used. Simple sentences are also used well, though more complex structures rely mainly on coordinating conjunctions. There are only occasional unimportant errors in spelling.

Task 2   Authentic Student Answer

While the rich countries of the world are getting richer, the poor nations are getting poorer to a level that the battle for survival is a non-ending routine way of life in some parts of the world. Moreover the gap is getting bigger in recent years. For various reasons the outcry for help is getting louder than ever before.

Lack of education is the main cause of poverty and famine in most parts of developing and poor countries. Children in school age are forced to work and get part in family income which is inadequate otherwise. In some parts of Africa and Asia children of age 7-12 are obliged to work in industries to help meet the family needs. There are some efforts from national governments to help their own people and from the international communities. The main way to help is to help improve the education of people. Giving just money and food are not the best ways. Education helps give people independence.

Climate change or global warming is another problem that the poor nations are facing the most. As a consequence, dry summers and lack of rain in some parts of Africa specially sub-Saharan Africa are turning the area into a battlefield where domestic cattle are lying dead in their thousands and crops are not growing. Water shortage forced people to leave everything and move to areas where water is or travel miles for drinking water every day to survive. Moreover torrential rains and flooding take life and homes of many people in my home country of Afghanistan. And the answer is to reduce the polution or carbon emissions produced by factories mostly in rich countries, which will reduce the threat of natural disasters.

As many pooper countries rely on their agriculture export products more than anything else, putting a ban or taxing such products will add to the poverty. The solution is fair trade and take away the subsidies to given to farmers in Europe and other western countries.

In conclusion, it is wise to say that the whole world is a big giant family living together and the suffering of one will take the smile from the face of the other. Helping each other should be the main priority.

Grade: 6.5

Ideas and evidence are logically organized and paragraphed, but the solutions and conclusion are not sufficiently developed. There is some effective use of cohesive devices, though more are desirable. A good range of vocabulary produces some precision and flexibility. Though sentence structures are varied, some basic grammatical errors occur.

p35   Speaking

Further practice and guidance (p36)

PART 1

1 (e) Where do you come from?

   (d) Describe the place where you were born.

   (c) Tell me about the main types of buildings there.

   (b) How easy is it to get to?

   (a) How have the buildings in your hometown changed since you were a child?

Note the adjectives. It is always useful to use adjectives to describe and then explain them with *because*. Example: 'My home city, Shanghai in China, is *modern, as/because* there are lots of skyscrapers there and many new factories.'

2   Possible questions

Travelling:
Describe the transport system in your country.

Tell me about the main types of transport in your country. What is travelling like in your country?

How easy is the transport system to use? How extensive is the system/transport system?

How have/has the types of transport/the transport system changed since you were a child?

Flowers:
Describe a flower from your country/that you like.

Tell me about the main types of flowers there are in your country. What are the flowers like in your country?

How important are flowers to you?

Have the types of flowers available changed since you were a child?

3   holidays: relaxing; exciting; fascinating; exhilarating; busy; hectic; interesting; stimulating

    walking: relaxing; healthy; beneficial; interesting; exciting; peaceful

PART 2

2 a   6, 8

   b   3, 4, 9

   c   7

   d   7

   e   1, 2, 5, 10

TEST TWO

p37 Listening Section 1

Questions 1–5

1   70

2   September 15th/15th September

3   Mandela Suite

4   3.30/9

5   PA5 7GJ

Questions 6–10

6   **40**: The number forty (stress on the first syllable) can be confused with fourteen (stress on the second syllable).

7   **29 33 81**: numbers are usually said in pairs or in threes: two nine three three (or double-three), eight one.

8   **tables and chairs**: Listen for the numbers. Note the plural in both cases.

9   **30/thirty**: the pound sign is already there so do not write *pounds*.

10 **damage and injury**: Listen for the numbers. Be careful with the spelling: the *e* on the end of *damage* and no plural.

p38–39 Listening Section 2

Questions 11–13

11 **C**: Listen for the words *green products*. the speaker says: ... *new 'green products' coming onto the market for the environmentally conscious*. Young people (B) and higher prices (A) are not mentioned.

12 **B**: The speaker says: ... *grass roofs as interest in sustainable ecological building has led to the greening of the rooftops of residential and commercial buildings around the world.* So he is talking about homes and other buildings (commercial buildings). Europe (A) is not mentioned and we don't know if grass roofs are used more on residential buildings than others.

13 **A**: The speaker mentions A twice: ...*insulation and drainage. Then on top of the insulation and drainage layer is added a final layer of soil* ... (B) and (C) are mentioned, but you need to concentrate until the words *insulation and drainage* occur.

Questions 14–18

14 **maintenance**: Listen for *advantages/benefits* or positive words. Always keep the headings in the table in mind. The words *in summer/cool* are the key words to listen for.

15 **unattractive**: Listen until the speaker finishes talking about the advantages (*biodiversity and water absorption*) and listen for words related to appearance (*look*).

16 **tidy**: once the speaker starts talking about the tiles listen for how they look.

17 **heat**: The key words to listen for are *summer* and then *absorption*.

18 **pricey**: Listen for the advantages and then the disadvantage introduced with the word *but*.

Questions 19 and 20

B and E in any order. Try to listen for *educating, competitions, celebrities, cost/cheapness* and *media* at the same time. Underline only these words, not the whole phrase, and listen for them or related words.

**Further practice and guidance
(p41)**

Recommendations

A   yes

B   yes

C   yes

D   no

E   no

F   yes

G   no

Things to avoid

1   B

2   E

3   A

4   C

5   D

---

p40 Listening Section 3

Questions 21–23

21 **electronic whiteboard**: Listen for the words: *going to* (planning), *use* and *present*. Note the answer begins with a vowel and is a noun or adjective + noun.

22 **back-up**: Again the answer is a noun. Listen for the words *power-point presentation*. The words *cover myself* do not fit here.

23 **specific background material**: You need to listen for the word *websites* and then what the speaker's purpose is for asking for the names.

Questions 24–28

24 **C**: Listen for the example and then be prepared for the first name. You can predict that most of the answers will be given by Dr Owen. When you look at A–G, underline *must read, recent articles, abstracts, links, references, useful, limited*. This will reduce what you have to look at as you listen. Dr Owen says *skim the abstracts* and then Karen says: *It cuts out having to read everything.*

25 **G**: Dr Owen is not very enthusiastic about this one: *If I remember it's not that useful. I would say that there are very few things that you need to read there.*

26 **B**: Listen for the name of the website and then the recommendation. Dr Owen says: *those that have come out in the last term or so.* (recent)

27 **F**: Listen for the words *helpful, beneficial* (useful) after the name of the site.

28 **D**: Listen for the name and Dr Owen's comment which comes immediately afterwards: *... trying out the links that it gives.*

Questions 29 and 30

29 and 30   A and B in either order. Listen for negative comments. Underline the noun in each alternative except for E. Listen as Dr Owen talks about the volume of information and her comments about visuals: *How much should I use? Avoid crowding the screen. If you have lots of information at one time.... But what about visuals?*

**Further practice and guidance
(p43)**

Questions 31–40

Key words

31 courses/full and part-time.

32 the information before *about the students and lecturers*; the word *about* – listen for this word or a synonym: *approximately.*

33 the sub-heading: *sponsorship; students, technicians*

34 workshops/facilities

35 main work/teaching

36 technological

37 specialist technicians

38 the sub-heading: *facilities/expert* and something to do with working (*employed*).

39 the sub-heading: research/the name *Dr Yu.*

40 *popular* or a synonym (attracts large numbers of people).

Grammar

31 adjective

32 number

33 noun (plural)

34 noun (singular)

35 noun (phrase) (singular)

36 adjective

37 (adjective) noun (plural)

38 nouns (both plural)

39 (verb in *-ing* form as adjective) noun (plural)

40 noun (plural)

Questions about the questions

31 no

32 yes

33 no

34 yes

35 yes

36 yes

37 yes

38 yes

39 yes

40 yes

p42 Listening Section 4

Questions 31–40

31 taught

32 21/twenty-one

33 lecturers

34 restoration

35 mechanism of printing

36 computer-literate

37 crash programmes/programs

38 restorers, conservationists

39 printing machines

40 applications

p44–58 Academic Reading

Further practice and guidance (p47)

1 yes

2 no

3 no

4   **1**   investigated/food sources

      2   sea-vegetables

      3   half – then look for a related number or quantity

      4   land/freshwater

      5   marine

5 no

6 yes – half

7 no

8 yes

9 yes

10 yes

p44–46 Reading Passage 1

Questions 1–5

1 **A**: Put a box around the characteristics A–D in the text. This then creates a frame, inside which you can scan for the words in 1–5. The words *investigated* and *food sources* help you to find the answer. The answer is in the first line of paragraph 4.

2 **D**: The term *sea-vegetables* is long and it has inverted commas around it, which help you to find it. Scan for the word without thinking about the meaning of the whole of the phrase A. The answer is in the first line of paragraph 2.

3 **C**: The answer is at the end of the first paragraph. The word *half* is connected with quantity.

4 **B**: The answer is in the first paragraph, fourth sentence. The adjective *terrestrial* means *land*.

5 **D**: The answer is in the first paragraph, fourth sentence.

Questions 6–9

6   **murlins**: Put a box around the names of the types of brown algae. The names in italics of the two types of algae help you to locate the relevant part of the text. The names are long which also helps. The answer is in the first sentence of the fourth paragraph: see also *known as*.

7   **(basic) grant**: The name *Forbairt* helps you. The answer is in the penultimate sntence of the fourth paragraph. Use the words in the table, *Research funded*, to help you.

8   **hybrids**: You need to go to the next paragraph and look for the reason why the research is taking place. As in the fourth paragraph, the reason is given after the funding body, *Marine Research Measure*, is mentioned (in the third sentence).

9   **cross-breeding (studies)**: Remember you are looking for an advantage (see the table). So as you look, scan for something good or positive. Look for the word *ideal* in the fifth sentence of the fifth paragraph.

Questions 10–13

10   **(it) stimulates reproduction**: Scan for the words *red light*. The answer is just after the answer for question 9. The word *do* tells you that a verb is required.

11   **relatively high**: The answer is in the sixth paragraph, sentence 3. The word *be* tells you that an adjective is required.

12   **development and investment**: The answer is in the last paragraph, the first sentence. The word *need* tells you that (a) noun(s) is/are required.

13   **catholic food tastes**: The answer is in the last paragraph, the last sentence. The word *what* tells you that a noun/noun phrase is required. You are looking for the cause of the greater consumption/use.

Further practice and guidance (p52)

Matching names and statements

1   yes

2   yes

3   **A**   EU directive

   B   old products/redesigned

   C   RoHS compliant product

   D   RoHS exempt

   E   planning and communications

   F   design engineers

   G   Pb-free systems

Summary completion

Adjectives:	hostile, friendly, big, basic, insignificant, numerous, important, small, recognised
Nouns:	requirement, variety, idea, increase, decline, need
Verbs:	decline, increase, solved, need, recognised

Word type

18   adjective

19   verb

20   adjective

21   adjective

22   verb

23   adjective

24   noun

Checklist questions 18–24

18   no

19   no

20   yes

21   yes

22   yes

23   yes

24   no

p48–52 Reading Passage 2

Questions 14–17

14 B: Once you have boxed the names, the answers are easier to find. The name *Manny Marcano* occurs several times in the text. Look at paragraph six; *including the need to redesign older products*.

15 C: In paragraph ten Stone says: ... *customer is going to choose a RoHS-compliant product*. The part of the text you have to look at is small.

16 E: This relates to Shultz in the ninth paragraph. Note this is not what he says, but what he is.

17 G: In paragraph five, you can see Stanvick is the one who talks about Pb-free.

Questions 18–24

18 C (hostile): The relevant part of the text is paragraph 1. See the word *unfriendly*.

19 J (decline): The relevant part of the text is paragraph 1. See the words *lost sales*.

20 F (basic): The relevant part of the text is paragraph 3. See: *Other countries, ... are creating their own 'green' or RoHS-like legislation. That means RoHS compliance must become an integral part*. Note the word *integral*.

21 H (numerous): The relevant part of the text is paragraph 4. See: *A host of technical and reliability issues remain to be sorted out ...* .The words *a host of* = numerous.

22 K (solved): The relevant part of the text is paragraph 4. See the words *sorted out*.

23 L (important): The relevant part of the text is paragraph 7. See: *'Previously, they looked at components based on size, performance ... . Now they have to add on a new constraint, ... environmental compliance.'*

24 A (requirement): The relevant part of the text is paragraph 7. See the word *constraint*.

Questions 25–27

25 True: The answer is in paragraph 8: *any country that can prove a product does not comply can levy fines against the vendor.*

26 False: The answer is in paragraph nine. It says: *will continue to be complacent ....*; this means they are complacent now, i.e. not taking the changeover (transition) seriously.

27 Not Given: The passage does not say when the directive will be introduced. See the last paragraph.

Further practice and guidance (p57–58)

Multiple choice questions

Question 34

1 yes

2 alternatives – cause; stem – effect

3 The last sentence of the first paragraph

4 *so ...* and *such ... that*

5 no

Question 35

1 Heading vii

2 **a** no

   b no

   c no

   d yes

3 yes

4 cause–alternatives; effect–stem

Question 36

1 Heading i

2 disparaged

3 B and D are not given. A is false.

Finding true statements

Questions 37–39

1	classroom	F and G
	equipment	E
	skills	NONE
	remote areas	F
	business	D

2 **A** yes

   B yes

   C no

   D no

   E no

   F yes

Global multiple choice question

Question 40

1 yes

2 no

3 no

p53–56 Reading Passage 3

Questions 28–33

28 iv: Look in the first paragraph for words that relate to *first*: *dawn of television, early, first*. The word *first* in the heading also gives you a clue. Look at the example heading (vii) for paragraph B. This tells you how something mentioned earlier developed.

29 i: The word *criticisms* in the heading shows what type of paragraph it is. Look for words which are negative. The word *disparage* (criticize, laugh at) may be unknown to you but there are other words that indicate the word is negative: *lack, can affect, camera conscious obstacles; former problem; hindered*.

30 vi: The words *How / benefits* tell you what type of paragraph it is. They show you the paragraph is organized around benefits. The plural shows there is more than one. Look for positive words: *enhanced, saving... time and money*. The prepositions, *through* and *by*, show the cause of the benefit. The rest of the paragraph gives other benefits.

31 viii: The phrase *various pieces* in the heading shows what type of paragraph you are looking for and the word *equipment* tells you the content of the paragraph. The paragraph lists different equipment: *ISDN lines, camera* etc. Heading v is not possible, because having two TVs is only part of the equipment.

32 ix: The word *lack* tells you that the paragraph is about something negative and *education* gives you the content. See the first line of the paragraph. Heading iii is not possible because it is not talking about 'transmitting' education by TV or radio.

33 ii: The word *future* gives you a clue that this may be the last paragraph. See the title of the passage and question 40.

Questions 34–36

34 A

35 D

36 C

Questions 37–39

37–39 **A, B, F** in any order.

Question 40

40 D

p59–63 Academic Writing

Further practice and guidance (p60)

Task 1

a The pie chart shows that the overwhelming majority of both sexes approved of the design.

b A greater proportion of women than men disliked the restaurants.

c Customers expressed their general satisfaction with the complex.

d There were more men than women who made no comment about the shops.

e Equal numbers of both sexes said they were unhappy with the shops.

f The data show the approval rating of various aspects of a new shopping centre in Auckland, New Zealand.

g Only 5 per cent of males were displeased with the restaurants compared to 21 per cent of females.

h It is significant that the restaurants received a more positive rating overall among men than women.

2 **i** an introduction **f**

   ii an overview **c**

   iii a comparison **b, d, e, g, h**

   iv a noticeable feature **a, h**

Note that **c** is the only overview of all the charts. Some sentences like **a** give an overview of one of the charts.

3 **1**   a

   2   h

   3   d

   4   e

Task 1 Authentic Student Answer

The tables and chart give the outcomes of a study carried out in 2006 about what people of male and female thought about aspects of a new shopping centre, constructed in Auckland, New Zealand. Both genders were asked whether or not they were happy with three things: shops, restaurants and design.

For shops, female respondents expressed greater satisfaction compared to males at a rate of 71% for women (34% very satisfied and 37% satisfied) against 61% for men (17% very satisfied and 45% satisfied). The impression of insatisfaction was the same for both genders (20%), while a twofold percentage of men (18%) compared to women (9%) did not expressed their satisfaction.

As can be seen for restaurants, a large number of men seemed to be satisfied at a percentage of 80 (25% very satisfied and 55% satisfied). The rate of happiness about restaurants was less for women compared to the other gender only 59% (with 27% very satisfied and 32% satisfied). There were almost four times more dissatisfied females than males (21% females against 5% males).

As regards design, the complex seemed to make a good impression on both genders with a high satisfaction rate, (62% satisfied, 17% very satisfied with only 10% dissatisfied and the remaining 11% not making any comment).

Overall, the majority of respondents were happy with the new shopping complex.

Word count: 224

Grade: 6.5

All parts of the prompt are covered, but the detail tends to be presented mechanically. The overview could be more fully developed. There is a fair range of vocabulary, but there is also repetition, with inappropriacies of style. Sentence structures are reasonably varied, with few errors.

Further practice and guidance (p62)

Task 2

1 Possible introduction:

In the last few decades, flying on holiday or business or for commercial reasons has become more popular than it has ever been before. As with all developments, such flights have brought both benefits and drawbacks.

Task 2 Authentic Student Answer

Nowadays people use more and more aeroplanes for holidays, business and commercial reasons. Besides numerous advantages offered by flights, lie some drawbacks which require to be highlighted.

By flying, life is becoming easier, because people travel long distances in a short time even from one continent to another. This time saving is great advantage for those who go to holidays or for businessmen. Delicate goods like exotic flowers can be easily exported. Both producers and consumers are then satisfied. The former are ensured that their products can easily reach the consumers to be sold because of the existence of aeroplanes. Consumers can also expect to receive products on time when they need them. Exotic flowers that lovers offer each others on Valentine's Day every 14th February is a great illustration of this.

Another particularity of flights is their convenience. This suitability attracts more travellers to use flights than other modes of transport. Despite all these benefits, flying is becoming a cause for concern.

One of the great problems caused by aeroplanes is the damage to the environment. By flying at high speed, they consume a great amount of fuel and they create a lot of noise which affects people living near airports. In matter of public health, aeroplanes can speed the spread of some epidemic diseases.

To sum up, flights which procure many facilities to people are also a cause of concern regarding the environment. In order to tackle this problem tough measures should be taken like huge tax increase to discourage people to use often aeroplanes. This money collected by the government could be used to repair the damage caused to the environment to save our planet for future generations.

Word Count: 281.

Grade: 6.5

Though the first paragraph adds nothing and follows the rubric too closely, the ideas are relevant and sufficient. Paragraphing is not well managed, though cohesive devices are generally well used. A good range of vocabulary gives flexibility and precision to the writing. Sentence structures are reasonably varied, without significant grammatical errors.

p62 Speaking

Further practice and guidance (p65)

PART 2

2   Model answer

I would like to talk about a time when I was late for an important job interview earlier in the year. The appointment was at 11am and I had got up early, as I wanted to be there on time. I set off by train several hours in advance; in fact, I caught the train before I needed to. Unfortunately, the train stopped just outside my destination, because something had happened on the line. I was becoming very nervous and was even worried about telephoning. I used my mobile to leave a message with the receptionist, but I was anxious that she might not pass it on to the interviewers. When I eventually arrived at the interview I was very uneasy and tense because I felt that I hadn't had time to prepare. I apologized to the interviewers, but I needn't have been so panicky, because they made me feel very relaxed. The appointment was important, because it was my first job interview.

PART 3

Question 1

Synonyms: crucial, vital, necessary, critical

Question 2

Adjectives: irritating, annoying, rude, frustrating, stressful

TEST THREE

p66–71 Listening

> **Further practice and guidance (p67)**
>
> **Questions 1–7**
>
> 1   c
>
> 2   c
>
> 3   b
>
> 4   b
>
> 5   a
>
> 6   a and c
>
> 7   c

p66 Listening Section 1

Questions 1–5

1   **3.5 kg/kilogrammes/kilograms**: This is heavy these days as the Union Rep says.

2   **(only) 0.5/nought point five GB/gigabytes**: The speaker says: *... only 0.5.*

3   **37.5 cm**: David says: *Well, mmm ... the screen is ... let's see, it's 37.5 cm.*

4   **2½**: David says: *The battery lasts for 2½ hours which is okay but not enough for long train journeys.*

5   **wireless**: The Union Rep again repeats the information: *Right. Okay. Not wireless.*

Questions 6–10

6   **scanner and headphones**: You can use your own knowledge to help you predict what equipment goes with computers. But always check that your prediction is correct.

7   **£300/Three hundred pounds**: Be careful with the numbers. The seller says: *It's worth about £900-£1000 new.* The Union Rep points out it's second hand. The Union Rep then says: *... So shall we say £300?* and David says: *Okay put that.*

8   **Bristow**: Be careful with the letters *P*, *B* and *R*.

9   **09875 42 33 87**. Remember the numbers are usually said in threes or twos: zero nine eight/seven five/four two/three three (or double three)/eight seven.

10   **22nd October**: Note the correct spelling of October.

p68 Listening Section 2

Questions 11 and 12

11   **permanent staff members**: Listen for the number 9. Be careful with the plural.

12   **(quick) tour**: The speaker says: *The main aim of the Open Day is to ... .*When you hear these words you know the answer is coming.

Questions 13–15

13   **oversee training**: Listen for the name and then for the responsibility of the person. Once you hear the name *Sean Bond* and his responsibility, you know you are about to hear the others. In this case, the speaker says: *Next we have Margaret Lloyd. Her main function is to ...*

14   **manage bookings**: *The next person is James Todd, who is: ... our Liaison Officer. What he does is ...*

15   **prevent injuries**: For the next person, Edward Marks, the speaker says: *His main role is to ...*

Questions 16–18

16   **E**:   In these three questions listen for the floor in each case and then afterwards comes the amenities. The speaker says: *On the ground floor there are ... with the shop and cafeteria over here ...*

17   **C**:   The speaker says: *On the first floor, we have a full range of fitness machines ... around which there are various offices.*

18   **B**:   The speaker says: *On the second floor, there is a series of small therapy rooms with waiting areas for clients.*

Questions 19 and 20

19   **3/three**: Check the other items on the table. This will help you predict the type of answer. In this case it is a number.

20 **Thursday 4.30**: Check the other items on the table. This will help you predict the type of answer. In this case it is a day and a time.

Further practice and guidance (p70)

1 a yes

   b yes

   c systematic

   d appearance

   e to a third

   f the order

   g rated too highly

   h yes

2

   23/24 Hand-outs: Mark probably says the hand-outs were good or something similar because Anna says they were the best part. However, the tutor makes a comment about reducing the length/volume by a percentage or a number: see the instructions.

   25/26 Middle of presentation: According to Mark, there was problem in the middle of the presentation where something went wrong with the slides. Anna then gives a reason for this, saying that they were over confident about something, and the tutor agrees that they need more practice with the equipment.

   27 Aims and objectives: Mark says something positive, very focused, and then Anna also gives a positive comment – they are clearly set out (arranged/presented). The tutor makes no comment.

   28/29 Delivery: Mark makes a comment about this and Anna states a problem. The tutor then suggests something. You can predict that Mark's comment was either neutral or negative.

   30 Score: Mark gives a number which is likely to be out of ten. Anna's mark is likely to be around the number six.

---

p69 Listening Section 3

Questions 21–30

21 **2nd December**: The word *Date* tells you what is required here.

22 **academic**: Use the heading on the table to the left to guide you. Listen for the tutor's question about what they thought overall and then Mark's comment that the presentation went well generally. Then listen for Anna's comment about what Mark says. The word *thorough* or a synonym follows this and prepares you for the answer.

23 **professional**: Use the heading on the table to the left to guide you. Listen carefully when Mark mentions the hand-outs.

24 **about a third**: After the two students comment on the hand-outs, the tutor then comments on the length and says : *Perhaps, you could have cut them by ...* .

25 **sequence**: Use the heading on the table to the left to guide you. You can perhaps predict the meaning but not the exact word. The word *order* might come to mind first.

26 **technical ability**: The tutor's comment gives you a clue that it is something technical. Listen for synonym of *overestimated: rated ... too highly*.

27 **set out**: Use the heading on the table to the left to guide you. You can perhaps predict the meaning not the exact words. When the words *aims and objectives* are said by the tutor and Mark has given his comment, be ready for Anna's.

28 **average**: Use the heading on the table to the left to guide you. When the tutor asks about this be ready for Mark's comment.

29 **most improvement**: After the two students have given their comments and the tutor gives some negative feedback listen for the words: *To me this is the area that requires ...*

30 **7/seven**: Use the heading on the table to the left to guide you.

p71 Listening Section 4

Questions 31–33

31 **A**: Listen when the speaker says: *We established the Centre in response to approaches from several business people ... Moreover, they had all without exception come up against ...* B is incorrect because it is the opposite. C is incorrect because although obstacles is mentioned, the speaker says: *...enormous bureaucratic obstacles* – we do not know how many.

32 **C**: Listen for the words *centre* and *focus*. The other two are incorrect because neither are mentioned.

33 **B**: Listen for *snapshot research* and *conducted*. The speaker does not mention the Internet (A) or personal contact (C).

Questions 34 and 35

34 **33/thirty-three %/per cent/percent**: Listen for: *The most common reasons given for the businesses closing were: first, high rents ...*

35 **2/two**: Listen for: *Since the centre came into existence three years ago, we have helped to change this climate of failure. The current statistics ...*

Questions 36–40

Use the headings, Size of business/Companies to guide you and then the size and names of each business. When they mention what the company is doing, listen for the support given afterwards.

36 stock

37 production targets

38 expansion plans

39 (company's) product range

40 team building

p72–86 Academic Reading

> ### Further practice and guidance (p76–77)
>
> ### Reading passage 1
>
> #### Question 4
> **1** yes **2** yes
>
> #### Question 5
> **1** yes **2** yes
>
> #### Question 6
> **1** yes **2** no
>
> #### Question 7
> **1** yes **2** several things (plural noun)
>
> #### Question 8
> yes
>
> #### Question 11
> **1** yes
>
> **2** no
>
> **3** yes
>
> **4** yes
>
> #### Question 12
> **1** yes
>
> **2** yes
>
> **3** yes
>
> #### Question 13
> **1** yes
>
> **2** no
>
> **3** yes
>
> **4** yes

p72–75 Reading Passage 1

Questions 1–3

1 **types**: The answer is in the second sentence of the first paragraph.

2 **tunnels**: The answer is at the end of the second sentence of the first paragraph. Note the number of words, so you cannot write the word *rough*.

3 **areas**: Look for the name, Te Kuiti Group. The answer is in the third sentence of the second paragraph.

Questions 4–8

4 **cracks**: The answers for the flow-chart are in the third paragraph. The answer is in the third sentence after the cause of the cracks: *the earth's movements*. Note the word limit throughout the chart, and remember that this is in note form.

5 **fractures**: The answer is in the following sentence. The word is related to the word *cracks* in 4.

6 **passage**: The answer is in the fifth sentence. Note the one word answer – no auxiliary, no article.

7 **streams**: The answer is in the fifth sentence.

8 **erosion**: the answer is in the penultimate sentence in the paragraph.

Questions 9 and 10

A and E in either order. B does not apply to all the caves. The answers are in the fourth paragraph. C is not possible because only some of them are vertical: *or high vertical water-worn shafts, ... Caves in the harder, massive Mount Arthur Marble (a metamorphosed limestone) are mainly vertical in development.* The word *vertical* earlier in the paragraph relates to a cross-section of the cave, i.e. a view from the side. As regards D, see the beginning of the paragraph: *... often with passages on several levels ... .*

Questions 11–13

11 **False**: The answer is in the first sentence of the second paragraph. Note how the questions here overlap. The key words to scan for are the numbers. The text gives information about limestone of all ages, not just one. The limestone in New Zealand therefore is not restricted to one period as in the statement. Be careful with the articles in **True/False/Not Given** exercises.

12 **True**: The answer is in the third sentence of the fifth paragraph. Scan for the word *stalactites* and then the colours. The comparison is in the words *usually* and *occasionally*.

13 **False**: The answer is in the fourth sentence from the end of the fifth paragraph. Scan for the word *stalagmites* and something to do with size. Note that you should not expect that there will always be a **Not Given** answer.

Further practice and guidance (p82)

Question 23

1 yes

2 yes

3 yes

4 no

Question 24

1 yes

2 yes

3 yes

4 yes

Question 25

1 yes

2 no

3 yes

4 yes

Question 26

1 yes

2 no

3 yes

4 no

p78–81 Reading Passage 2

Questions 14–18

14 C: The answer is in the third sentence of the first paragraph: A is not possible, because it is related to which hemisphere you are in. B also contradicts C. D is not possible because it was **reported** in the Daily Mail, not discovered by them.

15 B: The answer is in the third sentence of the second paragraph. It says: *Hereditary factors have been ruled out.* A, C and D contradict B.

16 A: The answer is in the last sentence of the second paragraph. B is not possible, because it is totally unknown rather than ambiguous. C is not possible, because Plato didn't work it out. D is not possible, because it is the opposite of A.

17 B: The answer is in the fourth sentence of the third paragraph. The passage says: *The non-judgmental term southpaw, by contrast, originates ...* . The term *southpaw* is not Anglo-Saxon. The statement contrasts with the other negative terms in the paragraph. So the other two are not possible.

18 D: The answer is in the fifth paragraph. A is not possible, because it contradicts D. B is not mentioned and neither is C. There is a mention of bird-flight, but not for many cultures.

Questions 19–22

19 Thomas Carlyle: The answer is in the fourth paragraph. Scan the passage for the name.

20 bird-flight: The answer is in second sentence of the fifth paragraph. Scan the text for the words: *ancient Romans/predict future*.

21 losing money: The answer is in the second sentence of the sixth paragraph. Scan the passage for *itchy palm*.

22 clockwise: The answer is in the last sentence of the sixth paragraph. Scan the passage for the words *wine/table*.

Questions 23–26

23 G: The answer is at the beginning of the seventh paragraph.

24 C: The answer is in the fourth and fifth sentences of the seventh paragraph.

25 F: The answer is in the last sentence of the seventh paragraph.

26 A: The answer is in the first sentence of the eighth paragraph.

Question 27

27 C: A, D, and E only refer to part of the article and it is not about B.

Further practice and guidance (p86)

Question 28

1 T

2 T

3 T

Question 29

1 T

2 T

3 F

Question 30

1 In the text two countries and Europe are mentioned.

2 The paragraph describes the part or role played by governments.

3 This is how the governments influence the professions.

Question 31

1 F: The word *client* is related to the word *professional* in the paragraph.

2 T

3 T

Question 32

1 T

2 T

3 F: Only the first part of the paragraph is about the lack of a clear definition.

p83–86 Reading Passage 3

Questions 28–32

28 F: Use the word *how* to give you the organization of the paragraph: ways/methods. Scan for the words *socio-cultural* and *developments* (or a synonym: *changes*). The paragraph describes different changes professionals have made.

29 D: Use the word *characteristics* to tell you what type of paragraph it is: examples of characteristics. Scan for the word or a synonym (*features*). Also look for words which indicate a list: *in addition/also*.

30 C: *Role* here gives you the clue; look for words like *shape, intervention*, etc. Scan for the words *governments/different countries*.

31 B: The paragraph describes how clients and professionals interact. The word *relationship* is not mentioned in the paragraph.

32 A: The answer is at the beginning of the paragraph.

Questions 33–37

33 (specialist) advice: Use the answer to 31 above to help you locate this. Questions 28 to 32 were general questions about the same passage.

34 academic institutions: Use the answer for 30 above to help you. Scan for the words: *US, liberal markets, impact* (or a synonym).

35 licence to practise: The answer is in the third sentence of paragraph D. Scan for the words *qualifications* and *experience*. The question relates to 29 above.

36 (long-term) decline: The answer is in paragraph E, the second sentence. Scan for the number 50 or a synonym: *half a century, from 1950* etc.

37 self-regulation: See the first word of paragraph G and the sentence before the last. Scan for *social and economic privileges*.

Questions 38–40

38 more open: The answers for these three questions are in paragraph F. See the fourth sentence.

39 demanding: See the fifth sentence.

40 specialisation: See the last sentence.

p87–91 Academic Writing

Further practice and guidance (p88 and 90–91)

Task 1

1 The best order is C A B

2 All of the verbs except for *fall* are used in the passive.

3 supply/send; pipe/send; purify/treat; clean/treat; carry/send

4 collection, storage, recycling, treatment, purification, supply

Task 1 Authentic Student Answer

The diagram show the way rainwater is collected and reused for domestic purposes.

When the rain falls, it increases the water in the dams and streams for a period of time. The water is pumped to a water treatment plant in order to produce drinking water. The purified water are released for the household consumption as drinking water. In the house water are used first of for drinking, then washing clothes, cleanings in the kitchen and gardens. Following that the household waste is sent back to the water treatment plant in order to make it fit for human consumption again.

When it rains, the rainwater running from the roofs of houses is also collected and stored in a water tank. The water cannot be used for drinking but can be used for other household purposes. Most of this water are used by many people for their garden.

Rainwater fall to the ground and is sent via drains to the river.

Word count: 160

Grade: 6

Most details are included, but there is no real overview. The order and paragraphing of ideas is mostly logical and vocabulary is adequate for the purpose. Sentence structure is adequate but limited and lacking flexibility. There are grammatical errors, which do not impede communication, but do attract the reader's attention unduly.

Further practice and guidance (p90–91)

Task 2

1 a yes b yes c no

2 a yes b yes c yes d no e yes f yes

3

Paragraph 1: However; This …; and so …

Paragraph 2: because; not only…but also…; For example, if; Moreover; when; As a result; so…that

Task 2 Authentic Student Answer

As human being, we got the capacity to be forged depending on which factors we are exposed to. External influences such as the Internet and TV on the one hand and politicians on the other are an example of this. However, in my opinion, the former has more great impact on us than the latter.

The human behaviour develops since childhood. At that stage we are likely to be in contact with the TV and now the Internet rather than politicians. For example, children usually watch cartoons on TV, where they copy good and bad behaviour. This therefore would impact on them, influencing and building up their personality.

It is not rare o discover that many of us chose our career like teaching or engineering because they enjoyed to watch movies or cartoons relating to this subject.

However, there is no doubt that politicians as well impact on us through their speech and campaign. But this is occurred in at a later stage in our life, after being shaped by the TV and the Internet. Most of time politicians adress their speech to a mature audience who have the ability to judge and to decide on their proposals and society plans. That is why children are not allowed to vote in opposite to adults. Certainly, because being underage they don't possess the sense of judgement to make a political choice.

In conclusion, for the reasons advanced above, I consider the Internet and the TV have a greater impact on us as a consequence of being around us from the earliest stages of our life. Politicians, on the other hand iterven only later when we acquire maturity from education and the media.

Word count: 281

Grade: 6.5

All parts of the prompt are covered, but the content is somewhat repetitive and needs further development. Organization and paragraphing is satisfactory, with a limited but effective use of links. Vocabulary is adequate for the purpose. However, both simple and complex sentences frequently contain grammatical errors which are quite obtrusive.

p92 Speaking

Further practice and guidance (p93)

PART 3

1 **b** better accommodation

    c more leisure time

    d more holidays

    e fewer injuries

    f fewer money problems

    g no problems with managers

TEST FOUR

p95 Listening Section 1

Questions 1–4

1   **C**: Listen for the words: *two types of membership/life-time membership*. Be careful about the order of the numbers.

2   **C**: The answer comes fairly closely after number 1. When you hear *ordinary membership*, listen carefully.

3   **B**: You can perhaps predict from the question that there is a discussion about week-day and week-end openings. Listen carefully when you hear the words: *week-days* and *opening times*.

4   **B**: Once the woman asks about the programme, listen for an adjective (*extensive*) to describe it. A is the opposite of B and C is not mentioned.

Questions 5–10

5   **Rochester**: Be careful with the name spelling, especially the ending.

6   **Stone Avenue**: Remember not to write the number as it is in the question. Be careful with the letter 'e' at the end of the words *Avenue* and *Stone*.

7   **MA7 4PQ**: Be careful with the numbers.

8   **6633**: You will normally hear the numbers in pairs: six six/three three/rather than sixty-six/thirty-three or double six/double three.

9   **(monthly) instalments**: Note the plural.

10 **fortnight**: Listen when the woman asks about bringing in a friend as a guest.

Further practice and guidance (p97)

Questions 11–20

11   … nothing/won't be charged anything …

12   … not have to/won't have to pay anything …

13   Beach Shop

---

14   square

15   later/will not meet earlier

16   not all/most/the majority …

17   … winners …; book-tokens/will not receive money …

18   … (specialist) apparatus/will not pay for specialist technicians

19   … badly-organized/not well organized

20   glass and plastic …/… will not be put

p96 Listening Section 2

Questions 11 and 12

B and D in any order. When the speaker mentions the word *changes*, listen carefully. Listen for the nouns in the list A–E and listen for the adjectives or their synonyms (for the word *free*: *without charge/will not have to pay*).

Questions 13–15

13   **shop**: When the speaker mentions the number of teams, listen for the name of the first which is the Beach Team. Follow through the information in the table. After the speaker mentions the litter, listen carefully.

14   **seating**: Immediately the speaker mentions the second team, listen for their purpose: *…will be responsible for setting out seating*.

15   **9.30**: The time is given after the meeting point is mentioned.

Questions 16–20

16   **A**: The speaker says: *On the whole, the judges will have had experience of judging before*. So not all the judges, but most of them will have experience. So C is wrong and B is not possible.

17   **B**: The winner will be given a cash prize, not vouchers (A). The two runners up will receive book tokens (C).

18 A: The purpose of the donation is: *to help fund much needed specialist apparatus* (equipment). B and C are not mentioned.

19 B: The speaker mentions last year's organization: *to help make sure the actual parking is more organized than last year, which was a mess*. This means there was a problem. A and C are not mentioned.

20 C: The speaker mentions that the bags are only for all the recyclable material, like glass and plastic, not all rubbish (A) and not food (B).

p98 Listening Section 3

Questions 21–23

21 B: When Mary asks about the exam, Adam replies: *Of the seven exams, ...* So A and C are incorrect.

22 A: Listen when Adam and then Mary mention the two essay papers. Adam says: *I don't think it's a good way of testing our theoretical medical knowledge*. So B is wrong as it mentions *practical* and C is the opposite of A.

23 C: Mary and Adam have a discussion about multiple-choice questions. Listen carefully when Mary says they disadvantage women. She then says: *Multiple-choice questions benefit men more than women. They are a male construct.* A is wrong because this is not mentioned and B says they benefit females not males.

Questions 24 and 25

B and E in any order. Listen when they start discussing the role-play. Be careful with A (*rest* not *test*). There is no mention of C and D.

Questions 26–30

26 prioritize/prioritise actions: With the summary, pick the key words to help you predict when the answer is coming. Listen first for *problem-solving* and then *working in groups of four*.

27 (four/4) examiners: Listen carefully when Adam asks if Mary felt comfortable with 'four examiners' watching.

28 listen: Listen carefully when Adam says: *The test doesn't just assess whether people can talk a lot. It's about ...* .

29 team: The answer comes immediately after number 28.

30 appeal: When Adam asks about the policy on re-sits, the answer is coming.

Further practice and guidance (p101)

Questions 31–40

31 correct

32 incorrect: The size is in relation to the world's total ocean area

33 correct

34 correct

35 correct

36 correct

37 correct

38 correct

39 correct

40 incorrect: The machines have already played their part by processing and collating.

---

p99–100 Listening Section 4

Questions 31–33

31 A: The speaker says: *the Indian Ocean is different from the two larger oceans in that it is landlocked to the north*. She does not say it is warmer (B) nor does she say it does not extend into cold regions (C).

32 B: Listen carefully when the speaker starts talking about figures. She says: *... the ocean constitutes approximately one-seventh of the earth's surface and about 20 per cent of the world's total ocean area*. The word one-seventh relates to the proportion of the total earth's total surface (seven in A). C is incorrect.

33 C: The speaker says: *Madagascar (and Sri Lanka)... structurally parts of the continents of Africa and Asia.* The Seychelles are mentioned in relation to submerged ridges (A). Mauritius and Reunion are volcanic cones (B).

Questions 34 and 35

34 acidity: Listen for the words *oceanographers* and *meteorologists.*

35 habitats, peoples: Listen for the words *assessment* and *impact.*

Questions 36–40

36 observing ice packs: When the speaker starts talking about the ship and the buoys, she is beginning to talk about the data collection and processing. Immediately after she mentions the number of buoys, she gives the answer.

37 size: Listen for the word *satellite.*

38 raw: When you hear the phrase: *here at the Institute,* listen for the type of data that is received.

39 bank: Listen for the phrase *constantly processed* shortly after the answer for number 38.

40 experts/centres: Both answers are correct. Listen for the word *collated* and then *analysis.*

p102–114 Academic Reading

Further practice and guidance (p106)

Question 1

The words are all related to strength/ toughness and lasting for a long time.

Question 2

The words relate to the production of a plaque.

Question 3

Yes. The words are linked to panels/groups of people meeting to consider suitability for selection of a plaque.

Question 4

The words are related to considering the conditions/criteria that need to be met for selection.

Question 5

The words relate to a house being honoured/ commemorated and what factors have to be considered first.

Question 6

The words talk about the past/start; there are dates and words like *first.*

p102–105 Reading Passage 1

Questions 1–6

1 H: The word *toughness* helps you find the paragraph. Paragraph H has several words and phrases which relate to the word.

2 E: Note this sentence relates to a fact in the paragraph rather than the whole paragraph. Look for *time* and anything to do with production. See the fourth sentence.

3 C: The name of the Panel in capital letters helps you find the correct paragraph. The vocabulary in the paragraph relates to the way the Panel operates: *representatives, considers* etc.

4 B: The word *conditions* shows there is more than one. Another word for conditions is *criteria*: things that people must meet. See the third sentence.

5 D: The words *factors* (reasons), *house* and *honour* (commemorate) help to locate the paragraph.

6 A: The words *first* and *started* are good clues.

Questions 7–10

7 Blue glaze: The answer is in paragraph G, third sentence.

8 characters: The answer is in paragraph G, the fourth sentence. Note the word *characters* refers to the letters of the inscription (second sentence).

9 border: The answer is in paragraph G, fourth sentence.

10 19.5 inches/ins; 495mm:The answer is in the last sentence of the paragraph.

Questions 11–13

11 True: The answer is in the first paragraph, the third sentence from the end. The GLC erected 262 plaques, and English Heritage has erected nearly 300, the last sentence.

12 Not Given: The answer is in paragraph C. The rejection of proposals is mentioned, but there is no mention of an explanation being given.

13 False: The sentence contradicts the first sentence of paragraph F: The exact form of the blue plaque, as we see it now, was a relatively late development.

Further practice and guidance (p111)

Paragraph headings

Question 14

classes: categories, types, kinds

Question 15

1   way: method; how ...; means

2   forecast: predict; project; anticipate; estimate

Question 16

forecast, prediction, assumption, projection, anticipation, estimation

Question 17

means; technique; test; examination

Question 18

no

Question 19

yes. self-response: first word of paragraph H.

---

p107–110 Reading Passage 2

Questions 14–19

14 ix: Always remember to check the examples first. See the last sentence of the paragraph: *classified/categories*.

15 ii: The key words are *way* (test), *forecast* (predict) and *future*.

16 viii: The key words here are: *way, subjective interests* and *future behaviour*. See the second sentence. Compare heading ii.

17 vii: The words *method* and *psychologists* help you to find the paragraph. See the first sentence. Note iii is not correct, as it is only a detail.

18 vi: Look for the word *intelligence*.

19 xi: Look for *self-response*, the first word in paragraph H; *self-report* in the fourth sentence of paragraph H. Heading v is not possible, as it is only a detail in the paragraph.

Questions 20–23

20 C: The answer is in the third sentence of paragraph B. Look for the words *published, on the market* and *validity and reliability*. You can expect this answer to be near the beginning of the passage. The stem is talking about tests in general. A is not mentioned; B contradicts C; and D is not mentioned.

21 B: The alternatives show you the question is to do with aptitude tests, paragraph D. See the second sentence. A contradicts B; the comparisons in C and D are not mentioned.

22 D: See paragraph E. The purpose of this type of test is given in the second sentence: *in order to make predictions about some future behavior or activity.* Note the American spelling of 'behaviour'.

23 A: See the first sentence of paragraph G.

Questions 24–26

24 No: See the end of paragraph G. Note the word *only*. The passage says: *the most commonly used*, which indicates others are used.

25 Yes: See the first sentence of paragraph H.

26 Not Given: The scale is mentioned in the middle of paragraph H, but there is no comparison between the scale and other techniques, and there is no mention of accuracy.

Question 27

27 D: See the first paragraph. The other three alternatives focus on parts of the text: see the last sentence of paragraph B – note the list of five categories.

p112–114 Reading Passage 3

Questions 28–31

28 C: Put a box around the four names as a first step. The answer is in the first sentence of paragraph nine. The words *scientific data* help you scan for the information.

29 F: See paragraph six. Scan for the words *nanoparticles* and *carbon, breathe in* (inhale) *brain* and *blood*.

30 G: See the last paragraph, the second sentence.

31 A: Matsuura is mentioned more than once. See the end of the third paragraph. Scan for *biotechnology*.

Questions 32–35

32 genetically modified organisms/GMOs: See the second paragraph, the second sentence. Scan for *(strong) public disapproval*.

33 scepticism: See the third paragraph, the penultimate sentence. Scan for the word *European(s)*.

34 absurd: See the fifth paragraph, the fourth sentence. Scan for *nanobots*.

35 ill-health: See the seventh paragraph, the fourth sentence. Scan for *photocopier toner*.

Questions 36–40

36 L comparable: An adjective is required. See the last sentence of the second paragraph, where nanotechnology and biotechnology are compared: *wondering whether nanotechnology ..... could be in for similar treatment*.

37 F latter: The sentence is about biotechnology, the latter of the two in the previous sentence.

38 G dangers: A negative noun is required. See the fifth sentence of the third paragraph: *risks*.

39 I advantages: A positive noun is required. Contrast this with *dangers* in 38. See *benefits* in the fifth paragraph.

40 K attitude: A noun is required. See the phrase *public opinion* in the second sentence of the fifth paragraph.

p115–118 Academic Writing

Further practice and guidance (p116)

Task 1

1 Corrected sentences:

a Generally speaking, men tend to be more/women tend to be less involved in managerial jobs like skilled trades, senior officials and professional occupations.

c Males and females work in (very) different areas of the job market.

d By contrast, women are more common/ men are less common in professions like sales and customer service and administrative posts.

e Men are ten times more likely than women to be employed in skilled trades and also more likely to be managers and senior officials. / Women are ten times less likely than men to be employed in skilled trades and also less likely to be managers and senior officials.

Task 1 Authentic student answer

The bar chart gives the proportions of the workforce by gender and type of work in the UK in the year 2005.

Overall, it appears that male workers did not chose to follow the same jobs as those taken by their female peers in the year 2005. The most noticeable difference is illustrated in the field of skilled trades, where men outnumbered women by ten to one, (approximately 20% against 2%). For managers and senior officials men are also dominant (about 18% against approximately 12% for women) and among proffessionals there are also more men than women (around 14% as opposed to about 12%). Also in the sector of processing, plant and machinary, there were far more men than women with the ratio being approximately six to one in favour of men, i.e. approximately 12% for men to around 2% for women.

On the other hand, in the field of personal service and also in sales and customer service, these occupations were dominated highly by women. For example, in the personal service sector, for example, there were more women by a ratio of approximately 8 to 1 (approximately 14% compared to around 2%).

Word count: 193

Grade: 7.5

Some data are omitted, but key points are mostly presented logically, and are suitably highlighted by cohesive devices. The range of vocabulary adds flexibility and precision. Sentence structures are varied and well managed, though there are some grammatical and spelling errors which do not affect communication.

Further practice and guidance (p118)

Task 2

Paragraph 1 possible answer

Some people feel that electronic books or e-books will become very popular, while others believe that the future of media such as books is safe. I agree more with the second group because I think people will find it difficult to give up using books and magazines etc. that they can touch.

Paragraph 2 possible answer

When people hold a book or a newspaper in their hands, they feel good, because a book is made from a naturally growing product, trees. However, if they have only a lifeless piece of electronic equipment or a screen on a computer to look at, they do not feel close to it. Moreover, books and magazines are attractive to look at compared to information on a screen. And so, I think printed media are here to stay for a long time yet. But I also think that with more and more newspapers and some books on line, it is impossible to stop e-books entering our lives.

Task 2 Authentic student answer

Recent decades have seen huge advances in technology on various levels. Unsurprisingly an increasing number of people think that the printed media as we know it shape- and form-wise, such as books and magazines will soon be history.

However, there are till those who believe that the familier forms of media such as this material that you are handling now, will never die out. Or, at least, it will live for generations to come.

Those who they believe that media in its current shape and form will inevitably disappear have may reasons for that. For example they argue that everything is now changing rapidly and there is no reason why the media as it exists today should be an exception, because it cannot remain static in a changing world. Technology is affecting every aspect of our lives and therefore publishers have to follow the trend to keep up with other fields by producing electronic books; otherwise, they will find themselves out of business.

Customers and readers in this case will also be looking for a more convenient, more reliable, more affordable and more modern services. Technology is undoubtedly proving day after day its capability to offer all these desirable qualities in one backage to satisfy them.

In the other camp, there are those who believe that the existing form of media is going to last for ever. They argue that in addition to the cost involved of accessing and using e-books, there are other factors to be taken into consideration like the sentimental relation between the reader and the book or newspaper itself. The feeling of turning the pages of a novel while you are lying on the bed or sitting on a long distance train journey. These things will never be easy for technology to replace no matter how far it can go.

In my opinion, sooner or later, e-books will replace the book and newspapers as we have known it since our first experience with the printed word. How long will it take before this becomes a reality? It is really very difficult to predict.

Word count: 347

Grade: 8

Ideas are well supported and presented logically, with skilfully managed paragraphing and cohesive devices. The text is enlivened by appropriately used rhetorical techniques. The wide range of vocabulary is used precisely, and with awareness of connotations. Occasional uncertainties in handling complex structures and minor spelling errors do not affect communication.

p119 Speaking

Further practice and guidance (p121)

PART 3

1   Students 1 and 2 answer:

   Do sportsmen and women make good role models for young people? Why? Why not?

   Student 3 answers:

   Do you think people are happy to stay in the same job for a long time these days?

2   1   e

   2   f

   3   a

   4   d

   5   b

   6   h

   7   g

   8   c

Listening scripts

TEST ONE   Section 1

Questions 1–4

Receptionist:	Good afternoon, Italiabreaks. My name's Margaret. How can I help you?
John:	Hi. I'd like to book a short break in Italy – hotel and flights combined.
Receptionist:	Anywhere in particular?
John:	Yes. Venice, if possible. We've been looking at some of your brochures and I want to check if you have any special deals.
Receptionist:	Right. Let's have a look and see what we've got. Right, mmm. Okay ... I've got the screen up. Can you just give me a few personal details?
John:	Sure.
Receptionist:	First, can I just take your name please and a contact telephone number?
John:	Certainly. It's John Framlington. That's F-R-A-M-L-I-N-G-T-O-N and I'll give you my mobile number ... I can't always remember it. ... Yes, here it is ... It's 07987 44 11 92.
Receptionist:	... 44 11 92.
John:	That's it.
Receptionist:	And how many people is it for?
John:	Just two adults.
Receptionist:	Okay. Any particular price range?
John:	It's our first wedding anniversary and ...
Receptionist:	Congratulations!
John:	Thank you. So we wanted somewhere nice, but not too expensive. We would like to make it something to remember. Maybe, in the medium price range.
Receptionist:	Okay. How many nights do you plan to stay?
John:	Five nights only. That gives us plenty of time to do sight-seeing and to relax.
Receptionist:	Right, that's five nights only. And what type of hotel?
John:	We initially thought of going for a five star, but that might be too expensive. So we've been looking at four star hotels.
Receptionist:	We've got quite a few in our brochure, but the one I would recommend is the Hotel Scotland. It's four star and I know there are rooms available because I have just made a booking for another client there.
John:	I didn't notice that one. I don't know how I didn't see it.
Receptionist:	It's easy to miss them. I've also stayed there myself as we sometimes have to go and check out the hotels and of all the ones I visited this was my favourite.
John:	Oh, right.

Questions 5–10

John:	What's the hotel like?
Receptionist:	It has a courtyard for breakfast. It's got 50 rooms. It's just been renovated and so it's very stylish.
John:	Is it in the brochure?
Receptionist:	It's on page 63.
John:	Ah yes! I can see it's right next to the railway station, ...mmm, but what appeals to me most of all is that the hotel's very convenient for all the water buses. And the idea of having a terrace with the room I really find very appealing. These are big plusses!

Receptionist:	It's probably the most central hotel we have. You might think it would be a bit noisy as it's in the main commuter area and a place where tourists go. But from experience I can assure you the hotel is very quiet. Most of the rooms are facing away from the main thoroughfare. Can you tell me when you'd like to leave?
John:	17th March coming back on the 22nd.
Receptionist:	Okay. I'll just check again if there are places available. Two adults sharing, Hotel Scotland. ... Yes. That's gone through.
John:	Okay. And how much is the break including flights?
Receptionist:	There's a special rate at the moment because it's off-season. For five nights, let's see, it's £716 for a double room and flights. That includes airport taxes, but not insurance.
John:	Each?
Receptionist:	No. For two adults sharing.
John:	That doesn't sound too bad at all. What reductions do you have at the moment?
Receptionist:	Well, if you make the booking before the 17th February you get a further 15% reduction subject to availability.
John:	That's a big saving.
Receptionist:	Yes. It makes the price very reasonable indeed. Do you need travel insurance?
John:	Yes I suppose we better had.
Receptionist:	For seven day cover for both of you it's £17. 88.
John:	Okay.
Receptionist:	Do you want to book today?
John:	I think we should, but can I just check with my wife? Can you hold the booking for me?
Receptionist:	I can hold it until 1pm.
John:	Okay. That's fine. I'll get back to you immediately.
Receptionist:	I'll just give you a reference for the reservation.
John:	Okay.
Receptionist:	It's FAPSJM15.
John:	Thanks. I'll get back to you as soon as I can and definitely before 1pm. This is too good an offer to miss.

TEST ONE   Section 2

Questions 11–13

Good afternoon, ladies and gentlemen, my name is Councillor Norma Boyd and welcome to this exhibition about the development of the old Paper Mill factory and gas works site, which has been lying unused for more than a decade. There has been pressure on the council to use the land to build a training centre and a small business park. However, we have been encouraged by local people to create an open area for the benefit of the community, providing much needed space for recreation.

And I now have pleasure in announcing that the plans for the creation of a park, to be called Park Royal, and for flats have now been approved. I am also pleased to announce that we have secured sponsorship from local organizations.

More detailed plans of the developments are available from the council website, details of which are in your pack. In the meantime, I'd just like to take you through the plan here on the screen.

Questions 14–20

If we start here at the bottom you can see Parkside Street, where the main entrance to the park is. On the left of the entrance, in the bottom left-hand corner of the plan, there will be a block of 40 studio flats. On the other side of the entrance there will be some workshops for local businesses. There will also be another entrance here on the top right which leads into Pear Street.

Here in the centre of the park we will have an ornamental lake with paths radiating north, south, east and west to the different areas of the park. In the top right-hand corner just by the Pear Street entrance, there will be a large sports area with two football pitches and four tennis and volley ball courts. Just here beside the pitches on the same side of the path will be an outdoor swimming pool.

Now, in the top left-hand corner, a walled flower garden is planned with a rockery and a water feature with walkways, seats and lots of shady areas for the summer. Next to this, a sculpture garden is also planned. Now let's see, just here below the walled garden there will be a grassy amphitheatre with a permanent covered stage for open-air concerts. We hope that local schools and colleges will use this theatre to showcase student work. In the bottom left-hand corner of the plan, you can see that above the block of flats there will be a play area for children and directly to the right of this just near the main entrance there will be a wild area. More trees will be planted here and in the middle will be built an educational centre for use by local schools to encourage children to take care of the wildlife and look after the trees and plants.

And finally in the bottom right-hand corner of the park will be a café, opening on to Pear Street.

And now for questions. If anyone would like to ask anything I and my colleagues are only too happy to oblige. Yes, the lady in the front row ...

TEST ONE   Section 3

Questions 21–25

Rosana:	Hi. My name is Rosana McClaren. Mmm. I'm a bit early, but I have an appointment to see the assistant Registrar, Andy Matthews, at 10am.
Andy:	Hi, I'm Andy Matthews. Nice to meet you.
Rosana:	Nice to meet you. My tutor advised me to come to see you about changing my course.
Andy:	Yes. I've had an email from your tutor, David Vine. Let me just call it up. ... Here we are. It says tutee ... Rosana McClaren ... is on the Wednesday part-time course and wants to change to the distance learning programme. Have you any problems with the course itself?
Rosana:	Oh no. I love it. I think the course is really worthwhile. The theoretical sessions once a week on Wednesday from 10am to 3pm are really good.
Andy:	You have two two-hour sessions then?
Rosana:	Yes that's it. And I have to say I think the practical session from 4 through to 9 in the fashion workshops are also good fun, but I am finding it all very tiring and it makes me too exhausted for my work on Thursdays and Fridays.
Andy:	You work the other four days of the week?
Rosana:	Yes, and some Saturdays.
Andy:	I see. So what do you want to do?
Rosana:	I'd like to change to the programme with the distance-learning component instead of the Wednesday sessions.
Andy:	Yes. That is a possibility. I see from your tutor Dr Vine that he has no problem with this, but you realise it's possible you'll have a different tutor.
Rosana:	Yes. I'm aware of that. It's a shame because he's a very good tutor. What do I need to do now?
Andy:	First, we just need you to fill in this transfer form and the claim form for the reduction in fees.
Rosana:	Oh. I didn't realise it was cheaper!
Andy:	Oh yes. It's a thousand pounds less a year!

Rosana:	It gets even better! Can I start the distance-learning programme from now?
Andy:	I don't see why not. I just need to get a signature from your tutor, which should take only a short time. I'll email it to him now and then he can sign it and put it in the internal mail.
Rosana:	Okay.
Andy:	But I also need to go through with you what is involved in the distance-learning programme to make sure you are clear about everything.
Rosana:	Well, I understand I attend the weekend course once a month and that I can book a bench in the fashion workshop at any other time.
Andy:	You have a computer at home for the distance-learning?
Rosana:	Oh yes. I have the necessary equipment for making video calls over the Internet already. It's the flexibility of the distance-learning over the Internet that is very useful. And what makes it even more interesting is that I don't have to spend a lot of time travelling to and from the university on the Wednesday. I can adapt it to my own routine, as I will be able to do the theory over the Internet from home when I want. The same is true of booking a tutorial on line using Skype.
Andy:	Yes it is amazing, isn't it? It's in its infancy but it's been up and running for a year now and it's going rather well.
Rosana:	Can I just ask if it's possible to have a face-to-face tutorial at any time as well?
Andy:	There is no reason why you shouldn't be able to.

Questions 26–30

Rosana:	What about the assessment for the distance-learning? I take it that it's the same as for the other programme?
Andy:	Let me see. Each month you are expected to keep a written course diary and to present a seminar paper and at the very end of the course there will be a written exam which will account for 30 per cent of the total marks.
Rosana:	What about the course work? How much does it account for?
Andy:	The design portfolio, which you need to present at the end, accounts for 50 per cent. I would point out just one thing and that is that on the distance-learning programme some tutors like to see the design portfolio twice each term to make sure you are on the right track. But of course you can take it in at any time to show your tutor. And as part of the assessment for the portfolio, you have to present at least one fashion item at a fashion show at the end of the course.
Rosana:	Is there anything else?
Andy:	No, that's it.
Rosana:	Thank you for all your help.
Andy:	No problem. Hope it all works out well for you now.

TEST ONE   Section 4

Questions 31–37

Student:

My group has been doing a project on the importance of architecture in people's lives and whether it has any impact on the lives of people in general. The main part I have played is in the collection of data to find out what effect, if any, various buildings have on people's mood, i.e. whether ugly buildings make people unhappy and whether beautiful buildings do the opposite.

We had originally thought of starting measuring people's reactions by using a questionnaire with about 40 questions, which we were going to hand out to people including students at the university. But we were worried that doing the questionnaire would be too time-consuming for people to fill in, so we gave up the idea. I then asked several of the postgraduate students for advice. One of them came up with the simple idea of showing people images of various buildings from different eras and styles instead of giving out the questionnaire and asking them to indicate how they felt on a scale of 1–5 about the images where 1 was unhappy and 5 was very happy. People would also be given the option of not saying what they felt. Using the scale meant that it would be much simpler to record people's reactions.

I decided to follow this advice and so the first stage was to collect a large number of images. I used Google to print off colour images of views of houses and apartment blocks where people live and different types of buildings where they work. I started with about 30 or 40 and then reduced them to ten images.

Media resources in the Amory Building at the Judd Street branch of the university helped me produce the final images. I had them blown up to A4 size and we used colour rather than black and white to make the detail on the images clearer. We made five sets of images and for protection when handling we pasted the images onto hard card. Then using a machine to wrap them with plastic we laminated the cards.

Five of us targeted different age groups; we went to a local school where we obtained permission to ask a group of teenagers between 11 and 18. We also asked a sample of the general public including tourists from all over the world, as they exited the Tate Modern in London, what they thought. We aimed to ask people from different age groups, namely 20 to 40 and 50 and over.

What our group learnt most from the project was first of all the value of teamwork. And secondly we found that we had to appoint a leader to stop us pulling in different directions and falling apart, so this turned out to be an invaluable lesson for all of us.

Questions 38–40

As to the findings, for us they proved intriguing. In the end the sample consisted of 311 respondents. I thought initially that people wouldn't be interested in taking part. With the youngest age group, their reaction was very mixed. It was clear that the youngest group had no pattern of preference at all, as they frequently gave no reaction to the pictures. For the 20–40 age-group, we found that they tended to score more in the middle range around 3.

We found that out of the three groups the most likely to be favourably affected by the images, that is, they were more likely to score the images as 5, were those aged 50 and above. And nobody in this age group failed to say what their reaction was, which was unique for the three groups. In total, I have to say that about 71 people indicated that they had no reaction at all to an image.

Our general conclusion is that we need to find out more about why people react as they do by perhaps giving them a chance to give reasons for their decisions. I would like to finish there and give my team-mates a chance to add anything I have missed, or take any questions or suggestions.

TEST TWO   Section 1

Questions 1–4

Man:	Hi. Good morning. My name's Pete. How can I help you?
Woman:	Hi. My name's Maria Lincoln. I understand you hire out rooms in the community centre as venues for parties.
Man:	Yes we do. We have various sized accommodation; it depends on what you're looking for really.
Woman:	We're looking to hold a party, ... a children's birthday party, and we need a room that will hold about 70 people with space for a small disco area, games, dancing, and food.
Man:	Well, we have a large room and it would certainly hold at least 100 people comfortably. It is used a lot for parties, things like that.
Woman:	Mmmm. That sounds as if it might be suitable. I've tried various venues and they are either booked up or they don't hold enough people.
Man:	Can you tell me when you were thinking of holding the party?
Woman:	I know it's short notice, but we wanted to hold it Saturday week, that's September 15th.
Man:	Let's have a look ... Mmm yes. You're in luck. The Mandela Suite is free then.
Woman:	I'll just write that down. M-A-N-D-E-L-A.
Man:	And the time? When were you thinking of holding it?
Woman:	In the afternoon from 3.30pm to 9pm.
Man:	Yes. Okay. There is no smoking on the premises and we are only licensed to have soft drinks.
Woman:	That's okay. I think I'm happy to go ahead.

Questions 5–10

Man:	Can you just give your postcode?
Woman:	Yes. It's PA5 7GJ.
Man:	Fine. And the flat and street number?
Woman:	It's Flat number 40, and the street number is 35.
Man:	Okay. So .... That's Flat 40, 35 Beeches Street.
Woman.	Yes, that's right.
Man:	And a contact number?
Woman:	My landline is 22 32 79 with the code. But I'll give you my mobile number which is 07897 29 33 81.
Man:	OK. ... 29 33 81.
Woman:	Mhmm. Can you tell me how much it will cost?
Man:	It's quite reasonable actually. It's £115 for the hire of the room, with tables and chairs, but if you want to hire disco equipment we've got a basic system with speakers and other equipment for £25, but there is no technician around in case anything goes wrong. And of course it's optional.
Woman:	That would save us carting something from home, but maybe we should bring a spare sound system just in case.
Man:	We have never had any problem with the system but you might not want to take any chances. What about catering?
Woman:	Well, we had thought of getting everyone bringing something.
Man:	We have someone who can do catering for £9 a head including the cake if required.
Woman:	That's handy, but it's a lot as we have a fairly tight budget.
Man:	So you want to go ahead with the booking?
Woman:	Yes certainly.

Man:	Okay. I need to take a deposit of £30, which is refundable. The balance needs to be paid two days before the event at the latest.
Woman:	Fine.
Man:	You can cancel up to two days before, but after that you lose the deposit.
Woman:	We don't intend to cancel, but is there any insurance we can take out?
Man:	Yes there is a form here somewhere.
Woman:	How much?
Man:	It's .... let me see it's only £9 for the 24-hour period and that covers you for cancellation, damage and injury.
Woman:	Well. At least we'd better have a look at it.
Man:	How would you like to pay the deposit?
Woman:	Cash.
Man:	I'll just give you a receipt.
Woman:	There you are. 10, 20, 30.
Man:	£30. Maria Lincoln.
Woman:	Thank you very much. I'm really glad I've found somewhere. We have been trying to book a place for the past two weeks. So thank you again and bye for now.

TEST TWO   Section 2

Questions 11–13

And now it's straight into the Eco Hotspot for today's programme. We are in fact going to look at an intriguing trend in recent years in the world of eco-friendly developments. There has been a constant stream of new 'green products' coming onto the market for the environmentally conscious. A new departure, which I feel needs greater attention drawn to it, is the increasing interest in grass roofs.

Environmentalists sing the praises of grass roofs as interest in sustainable ecological building has led to the greening of the rooftops of residential and commercial buildings around the world. And what does this type of roof consist of? Instead of tiles which allow water to run off and create flash flooding, the roof has a waterproof underlay which is laid over the roof deck. This waterproof layer is then covered with layers for insulation and drainage. Then on top of the insulation and drainage layer is added a final layer of soil or crushed stones for the plants and/or grass to grow on. The roof can be planted with wild flowers to add colour and life to your rooftop.

Questions 14–20

As for the benefits of grass roofs, in spring and in summer they are very pretty as flowers spring into bloom. Moreover, in summer grass roofs are of particular benefit in cities because they keep any building cool by reflecting the sun's rays. In winter the grass roofs insulate the building, helping to prevent heat loss. The roofs require little maintenance and are better than any other roofing material. They encourage biodiversity by attracting bees and birds and they absorb water run off which helps prevent flash flooding. In fact, the gravel layer retains 71 percent of the rainwater that falls, thus helping to prevent flash flooding. In winter, the brown soil is a bit more evident, which can look unattractive, if the roofs are not tended carefully, but that is a price worth paying and I would say that they come highly recommended by those who have them.

If you compare grass roofs with tiles, the latter do certainly look very tidy, but at a price to the future of the planet. The main drawbacks of tiles though are the water run-off and the absorption of heat from the sun's rays in summer. So if we are to save the planet from the ecological point of view, tiles do not come recommended. The only roof that I can think of which has similar ecological credentials to the grass roof is the thatched roof. Thatched roofs are good insulators and very attractive, but very pricey and not ideal for cities.

How can we make more of our roofs green? That is, how can people be persuaded to install grass roofs? The World Green Roof Conference in Australia was a very good start. At a grassroots level, the best way to raise the profile of grass roofs is to make them trendy by highlighting them in fashionable magazines so that people begin to feel that they cannot do without them. But the idea I like best is holding competitions for the best designed grass roofs.

Next week Eco-Hotspot is going to look at .... .

TEST TWO   Section 3

Questions 21–23

Karen: Excuse me Dr Owen, I ....

Dr Owen: Oh hello Karen.

Karen: Have you got a few moments?

Dr Owen: Yeah. Sure. How can I help you?

Karen: Well, I've had difficulty finding data on the original question and I was wondering if I could change my paper to "Investment in knowledge" comparing some European countries with the United States and then with others throughout the world including the OECD average. I've found lots of data by way of graphs etc.

Dr Owen: Where did you get the data from?

Karen: From various sources, books and journals.

Dr Owen: How are you going to present the material?

Karen: I am going to use the electronic whiteboard as suggested and do a blend of graphs, pictures, text and podcasts to illustrate my presentation.

Dr Owen: It sounds very impressive.

Karen: Yes. Let's hope the whiteboard works, but I'm also going to have a power-point presentation for a back-up – just to cover myself.

Dr Owen: A back-up is a good idea, but it's a lot of work doing everything twice.

Karen: It is, but at least I'll have experience of both.
            Before we talk about how to use the data I've selected, could you give me the names of a few websites I should look at for more specific background material? When you type in anything to do with knowledge there are millions of sites listed.

Questions 24–30

Dr Owen: Let's see. ... I'll print you off this list. .... There we go.

Karen: Right. Do I really need to study everything on these?

Dr Owen: No. I suggest there are five or six you can look at. The one you have to go through is the IT department section on the university site, which is www. kmul.org. It has articles by all of us in the department and has links to useful information. So I think it is essential to look at this.

Karen: Okay. I've already been on it, but I'll tick that one as a must read.

Dr Owen: And there's a site, which is hosted by Pollock, it's investment_IT.com. All you need to do is to skim the abstracts of the articles on the site; they'll give you a general idea about the effects of investment in knowledge.

Karen: Yes. That sounds good. It cuts out having to read everything. What about this one, knowledge_journal.com?

Dr Owen: If I remember it's not that useful. I would say that there are very few things that you need to read there. Then there's IT_ knowledge_review.com. It's got loads of articles, but it's probably best just to read those that have come out in the last term or so.

Karen: Do you have to subscribe?

Dr Owen: No. It's free from the university library. And another free journal on line is IT_online.com. I wouldn't say it's essential to read it, but it is beneficial and so I think it is worth a look.

Karen: If you think it's useful, there is no harm in looking at it.

Dr Owen: But NationalStatistics.com is worth looking at and trying out the links that it gives. I think these are probably enough to be getting on with.

Karen: I think so. There's another thing I want to ask about. How much material should I use in my presentation?

Dr Owen: Avoid crowding the screen. If you have lots of information at one time, people will not be able to follow it and will just switch off.

Karen: That's worth remembering. I've been in lectures where there was too much detail on the screen and it was impossible to read quickly. But what about visuals? Do you think it's okay to mix visuals and text?

Dr Owen: Visuals are very useful, but they must be relevant or else people will get confused about what they mean and why they are there. And they won't pay attention to what you are saying. So be careful. From what I can see you have the makings of a very good presentation.

Karen: Thank you!

TEST TWO   Section 4

Questions 31–37

I am here to give you a brief outline of the work of this new department. The Department of the Printed Word has a very short history, having been created just ten years ago. Some statistics to start with. The first intake of undergraduate students consisted of 20 students, which rose to 37 in the second year and we now have about 50 in the first year, doing a wide range of courses, full and part-time. We have a thriving research department with 17 students on the taught MA course and 7 students doing research full-time. In all we have 9 full-time lecturers and 16 part-time lecturers who work mainly but not exclusively in our evening department. Of the total student body, approximately 21 percent are from outside the country, a number which has been increasing steadily over recent years.

Although students from overseas have to reach a minimum level of competence in English before they follow a course at the university, some may require remedial help with their English and we can offer help through the Student Support Services as part of the general assistance given to all students. For home students, both graduate and undergraduate, there are bursaries to help with travel and accommodation, for which I would advise you to contact Mrs Riley at the end of this session.

Increasingly, we are forging external links with organizations in the publishing world. And we have been very fortunate in that we have received money to sponsor not just various students within the department but also technicians and lecturers. Each year we hold a series of lectures, which are given by external speakers in the world of printing and the media. The series of workshops that you see around you have been built thanks to a very generous donation which has allowed us to develop our facilities for book binding and restoration.

Now the main work of the department relates to teaching the mechanism of printing and as most printing is now so highly technological, all our students have to be computer-literate. For those of you who are interested in taking a module in this department from another department and who feel that you may not have the necessary computer skills, don't let the technology put you off. We have a number of specialist technicians who can support and deliver crash programmes in the computing technology required. As long as you can switch on the computer you are half way there.

Questions 38–40

We have what can only be called state-of-the-art facilities especially for those wishing to move into the publishing world working not just as printers, but also in editing, page design, layout and book-binding. With the extensive facilities we have for book restoration, some of our former students are now employed as expert book restorers and conservationists, skills which were once almost dying out. In the display you will notice samples of work on book cover design, and as well as having all the necessary computer programmes for dealing with printing we have some old printing presses.

Despite being largely a modern department, we do have an increasing interest in research into the history of the printed word, ranging from early European to Chinese and Japanese printing techniques. We have in fact some very well-known experts on early printing in Europe in the 15th and 16th centuries. If this area appeals to you, you can talk to Dr Fred Clare afterwards. From China we are lucky to have as a visiting lecturer Dr Yu, who is an authority on early Chinese manuscripts and printing machines. If you are thinking about doing a module with us or you are interested in doing research after you have finished your first degree, the person to talk to is Professor Clarkson who will be able to give you all the details. For postgraduate research, you should really be thinking about applying now even though we are only in December, as the department now attracts large numbers of people and we always have many applications for each research position.

TEST THREE   Section 1

Questions 1–5

Union Rep:	Hi. I'm Debbie. How can I help?
David:	Hi. My name's David. I'm just looking to place an advertisement on the main Union notice-board to sell a laptop and a few accessories, if that's possible.
Union Rep:	Sure. That's not a problem. I take it you are a member of the Students' Union?
David:	Yes, I am.
Union Rep:	Right then. I'll just get a form up and as there is no one around and it looks as if it's going to be quiet for a while, I'll just type the details straight into the computer for you.
David:	Thanks very much.
Union Rep:	No problem. Shall we just title it Laptop for Sale?
David:	Yeah OK.
Union Rep:	Can you describe it generally?
David:	Well, it's in very good condition; in fact it's hardly been used.
Union Rep:	Why are you selling it, if I may ask?
David:	Well, I've got another one which is much lighter and I don't really need two.
Union Rep:	I see. What weight is the one you are selling?
David:	It's 3.5 kilogrammes.
Union Rep:	That is heavy these days. Can you give more details about the one you want to sell?
David:	Right. Mmm. Well, It's an Allegro and it's got all the latest programmes.
Union Rep:	Okay. What about the memory?

David:	The memory is only 0.5 Giga-bytes.
Union Rep:	And what about the screen size and the other features?
David:	Well, mmm ... the screen is ... let's see, it's ... mmm ... 37.5cm with a standard size keyboard and a touch pad, but I've got a cordless mouse that I can put in with it if necessary. Some people don't like using a touch pad.
Union Rep:	What about ports or holes for attaching things to the laptop?
David:	It's got two ports.
Union Rep:	Mmm. More modern laptops have more than two ports for all the extra attachments.
David:	They do. Let's see what else is important? Oh yeah. The battery lasts for 2½ hours, which is okay but not enough for long train journeys. But one thing is that it's not wireless.
Union Rep:	Right. Okay. Not wireless.

Questions 6–10

Union Rep:	Anything else I can put on the advertisement?
David:	There's a web cam built at the top of the screen and I can throw in a printer, a scanner and headphones, which I got with it in a special deal. It also comes with its own case for carrying it around. Actually the case is quite smart. I'm hoping these things will help it sell.
Union Rep:	They should do. Right. I think I've got all that. How much do you want for it?
David:	That I'm not sure about. It's worth about £900-£1000 new.
Union Rep:	Yeah, but you won't get that much if it's used and even if it's in good condition.
David:	What about £500?

Union Rep:	I doubt if you'd get as much as that. More like £200 or £300. If you look at the notice board there is one on there which is comparable to yours and it's not more than about £250, I think.
David:	As little as that?
Union Rep:	I'm afraid so. Shall we say £300?
David:	Okay put that.
Union Rep:	Can I take some contact details for the advert?
David:	The name's David Bristow.
Union Rep:	B-R-I-S-T-O-W.
David:	Yes that's it, and a mobile or email?
Union Rep:	Both if you want.
David:	It's DIB_7791@hotmail.com
Union Rep:	Okay and the mobile?
David:	That's 09875 42 33 87.
Union Rep:	That's it. If you send the picture, I'll add it and print it out and stick it up for you.
David:	Okay, I can get that to you today.
Union rep:	Right. I'll type in here: Advert placed: the 22nd October. Fine, and good luck with the sale!
David:	Thanks.

TEST THREE   Section 2

Questions 11–15

Good morning, and welcome to the Open Day of our new Alternative Health Club, here at Chelsea Bridge. I have to say it is very pleasant to have so many people turn up. My name is Harry Wilkinson and I work as one of the nine permanent staff members employed here at the Club.

The main aim of the Open Day is to give you a quick tour of the building, but before we do that I'd like to introduce you to a few people employed at the Club. Not all of us are here at the same time. In case you need to contact any of us our contact details are here on the notice-board below the photographs. First of all, this is Sean

Bond, who is the Technical Manager and his job is to supervise equipment, like computers and all the electrical equipment. And this is Margaret Lloyd. Her main function is to oversee training and she is therefore in charge of all the full-and part-time therapists. The next important person I need to introduce you to is James Todd. He is our Liaison Officer. What he does is manage bookings for the Club rooms and equipment, as they are open to different organizations, from the local College to corporate clients like banks and so on.

Last but not least is our physiotherapist, Edward Marks, who works part-time Monday, Wednesday and Friday. Edward plays an important part in the life of the Club. His main role is to prevent injuries.

Questions 16–20

Now for the various amenities. You see that the Club has quite a large capacity and is arranged over three floors. There is a lift by the Reception and the stairs. On the ground floor, there are two large halls, which are used for yoga, Tai Chi, Pilates and dance and fitness classes for different age groups, with the shop and cafeteria over here. On the first floor, we have a full range of fitness machines, which are available in the large central hall, around which there are various offices. The changing rooms are also on this floor. On the second floor, there is a series of small therapy rooms with waiting areas for clients. These may be booked by individual therapists. There are also three classrooms, which are used for teacher training and group therapy classes.

We have a very extensive therapy training programme accredited to the university of Manwich with training in counselling, for which we have three programmes at the moment. As regards the various types of yoga, acupuncture and the Alexander Technique, there are currently nine different training classes going on. Information about the training can be obtained from the brochure, which you can pick up at Reception, and from the Club website. There will be a chance to talk to trainers for those interested in counselling this Saturday at 10 am. For yoga etc, there will also be an informal gathering of trainers on Thursday at 4.30 pm. So if you are interested in becoming involved, this is your chance.

TEST THREE   Section 3

Questions 21–26

Tutor:	Now, Mark, and Anna, I have to say that I thoroughly enjoyed your joint presentation on the application of robotics in a non-industrial setting to the group on 2nd December and it is clear that you have both devoted quite a lot of time and effort to it. Have you had a chance to fill in the self-evaluation form for the session?
Mark:	Yes, we have.
Tutor:	So Mark, what do you think overall?
Mark:	Well, generally, I felt the presentation worked very well; in fact, we seemed to hold the attention of the others throughout. And the pace of delivery was fairly even as were the range of activities we organized.
Anna:	I agree with Mark, but I'm not sure we were comprehensive or academic enough.
Tutor:	No comment really except that I don't think there was any question of it not being thorough.
Anna:	I think we were a bit too chatty and too joky at times rather than formal.
Tutor:	Okay. What do you think were the best areas and which do think can be improved on?
Mark:	Everything could have been improved on. I felt very good about the hand-outs; we had spent a lot of time putting them together. They had a very professional appearance as we bound them into a booklet.
Anna:	To me the hand-outs were the best part as we had a very extensive bibliography and the booklet seemed to go down well.
Tutor:	The booklet you did for the hand-outs certainly showed you had done a lot of work. But I think that you put too much material into it and people got distracted by it. Perhaps, you could have cut the hand-outs by about a third.
Mark:	I see. When I come to think about it, maybe you are right.
Anna:	Okay.
Mark:	But there were times in the middle of the presentation where things did go a bit astray. I think that was my fault when I got the power-point slides out of sequence and I had difficulty getting back on track.
Anna:	Mmmm. I also think we rated our technical ability too highly especially when operating under pressure. I had never done a presentation with technical equipment before, so it was a steep learning curve for me in particular.
Tutor:	Yes, I think you could have done with a bit more practice with the equipment beforehand.

Questions 27–30

Tutor:	What about the next item on the feedback form? The aims and objectives?
Mark:	I think they were very focused and we followed them through well, I think. We wanted to show how Europe was lagging behind other areas of the world.
Anna:	Yeah, I think they were clearly set out.
Tutor:	Yes. Agreed. No comment there.
Mark:	The diagrams and charts were appropriate.
Anna	Yes. I have put that too.
Tutor:	They did work well in helping to illustrate and break up the presentation by cutting down on the number of words and text on the screen.

Tutor:	What about delivery?
Mark:	Well, I think our performance was average.
Anna:	It was difficult to coordinate speaking and presenting the material at the same time. I was quite self-conscious of what I was doing. It was down to a lack of experience.
Tutor:	Unfortunately, both of you had the habit of standing in front of the projector so you kept blocking the image on the screen. To me this is the area that requires the most improvement.
Mark:	The section on the predictions of the commercial application in the future, I think appeared a bit haphazard. To me it was a weak point of the presentation. And I think that some of the slides could have had fewer words.
Anna:	And we could have done some fancy graphics with the words.
Tutor:	If you had to give yourselves a mark overall how much would you give out of 10?
Mark:	Six maybe. I would be happy with that, though bits were probably nearer a seven. So I'd say a six. Anna, what do you think?
Anna:	I think for me it's perhaps a seven.
Tutor:	Okay. Did you find the task and the evaluation useful?
Anna:	I think ...

TEST THREE   Section 4

Questions 31–35

The subject of this evening's talk at the North Bank Business Centre is local businesses in the area surrounding the university, and the benefit they bring to the employment prospects of people in the local area, especially young people at the beginning of their career.

We established the Centre in response to approaches from several business people in the area who had wanted to start up new businesses, but who had not managed to find any help locally and did not know where to turn. Moreover, they had all without exception come up against enormous bureaucratic obstacles. We therefore invited them in as a group to meet the members of the department and the students. Stemming from that is the Centre, which now focuses mainly but not exclusively on business start-ups.

Just after the Centre was set up, snapshot research conducted by the department over the telephone gave some startling results. The information about local businesses revealed that three out of every ten local business start-ups, that we could collect information on, had failed within the first six months, and another five had gone within the year, leaving only two. The most common reasons given for the businesses closing were: first, high rents, which are 33% higher than the national average due to the area being very central; second, lack of knowledge about grants, basically because of ignorance about how to access them; and thirdly a lack of business support, because they did not know where to obtain advice from.

Since the Centre came into existence three years ago, we have helped to change this climate of failure. The current statistics show a remarkable turnaround in the fortunes of local businesses. And now, after a year, only two businesses close out of every ten compared to eight before the Centre was set up.

Questions 36–40

Six local businesses are now taking part in a work-placement and monitoring scheme, which is of mutual benefit to ourselves and the companies involved. O-foods, a small start-up company with nine employees involved in organic food and based at a local market, has one final year graduate doing a year-long study on improving the stock turnaround. This was a particular problem because the company found that they were losing sometimes up to 30 percent of their stock. Another start-up is Innovations which deals with producing video games. This company, which employs only five people all under the age of 25, is receiving support in attracting business partners and achieving production targets.

In the smaller business category, Sampsons Ltd, a courier company, which is interested in developing a taxi service, is being offered help with their business expansion plans. Another small niche company, called Vintage Scooter, which specializes in revamping old scooters, is taking part in a product-monitoring scheme, offering customer service up to a year after purchase to check the quality of their restoration.

The first of the two medium-sized companies that the scheme is monitoring is Build Ltd, which employs 47 people. A comparison of their products and services with other businesses in the area is being carried out by a researcher, who is trying to support them in their efforts to extend the company's product range.

The last company, Jones Systems, is perhaps the most interesting, because it has been the victim of considerable personnel problems, which have been affecting the day-to-day operations of the company. And so we are looking at conflict management and team building within the company.

To sum up, advisors help the companies look at different business options and models, apply for grants, deal with employment issues, systems creation, and also provide accommodation at the centre to help them start up. E-mentoring for fledgling businesses is also in operation for those who find it difficult to attend the centre personally. The programme is funded by grants from local authorities.

TEST FOUR   Section 1

Questions 1–4

Woman: Hi. I'd like some information about joining the International Arts Society.

Man: That's no problem. What exactly can I help you with?

Woman: First of all, I'd like to know about the membership fee.

Man: Well, there are two types of membership.

Woman: Can you tell me what they are?

Man: First, there is life-time membership which means that you can have access to all the facilities at the society itself and all exhibitions. Plus you can have discounts to various events at affiliated arts organizations here and abroad. And on top of that you can use the life-time members' room.

Woman: How much is that type of membership?

Man: Well, the life-time membership fee is £1,537.

Woman: Mmm. Okay. It's rather a lot to pay in one go. What about the other membership?

Man: The ordinary membership; that's £193 per year.

Woman: That sounds a bit more reasonable. What does that entitle you to?

Man: You can visit the society, including the exhibitions, the library and follow the arts programmes on week-days during the opening times from 10am to 9pm and at the week-end between 10am and 5pm. On Saturday, if there is a special event like a lecture or restricted showing of an exhibition, then it opens until 9pm.

Woman: So what is the difference between this and the life-time membership?

Man: In the long-run, you save money as you are making a one-off payment, and you have exclusive use of the life-time members' room.

Woman: Okay. What arts programmes do you run?

Man: Well, the Society has a very extensive programme to cater for all tastes. There's a series of exhibition rooms for the permanent collection of paintings, watercolours and sculpture and then there's a new exhibition area, which opened at the beginning of the year. And we run a series of courses and lectures that go with the exhibitions.

Woman: Can I ask about the lectures? What is scheduled for this year?

Man: The latest list is in this leaflet.

Woman: Oh yes, that looks very good. Are all the exhibitions etc. free if I join?

Man: Yes. Everything is free.

Woman: That's fair enough. I think, in that case, I'll join.

Questions 5–10

Man: I just need to take your name, address and telephone number. First, your name?

Woman: Margaret Rochester.

Man: I take it that's R-O-C-H-E-S-T-E-R?

Woman: Yes, that's it.

Man: And the address?

Woman: It's 55 Stone Avenue.

Man: Okay ..... Avenue. And the post-code?

Woman: Mmm. Let's see. It's MA7 4PQ.

Man: And a day-time telephone number?

Woman:	Can I give you my work number?
Man:	Yeah. That's fine.
Woman:	It's 0207 895 2220 and the extension is 6633. Can I pay by credit card?
Man:	Yes of course. Do you want to pay for the full year at one time or by monthly instalments? You pay £4 extra a month if you pay by instalments.
Woman:	Okay. I think I'll pay by monthly instalments.
Man:	Right. If you just complete this form, ... then we can set up the monthly payments. .... Okay. If you just put your pin number in the machine, I can deduct the first month's payment. ... Right. That's gone through. Here's your card. I now just need to take your photograph over here and then I can put it on your membership card.
Woman:	Okay.
Man:	That's it. I'll just print out your membership card. Right. Here you are.
Woman:	Thank you. By the way, can I bring any friends to the Society exhibitions and lectures?
Man:	With the ordinary membership, we can issue a day pass once a fortnight which allows you to bring a friend in, but you have to accompany them.
Woman:	Thank you. Can I go in now?
Man:	Yes. You just swipe your card here.

TEST FOUR   Section 2

Questions 11–15

And now for the preparation plans for the town's 250th anniversary celebrations. We are going to follow the same system we had last year, but with a few changes to increase the party spirit.

First of all, this time we are going to make the concert on the beach open to everyone without charge. This is because we have been given money by the council for the celebration and also because last year we had so many problems with keeping people out who had not paid. And on top of this, people will not have to pay for refreshments either, as these are being donated.

Right now, mmm, we are going to divide into four teams: the first one, the Beach Team, will be responsible for cleaning up the beach on the Saturday morning, picking up litter, bottles, plastic bags, wood and anything else that's lying around. Everyone is meeting at the Beach Shop at 8 am. It's an early start, but we want to give everywhere a good thorough clean. We have had permission from the council to close the beach to get it ready for the anniversary celebration on Sunday.

The second team will be responsible for setting out seating in the square for the speeches and prize giving. Again an early start is preferable, but the vans with the seats can't be there until 9 am, so shall we say that everyone should meet at the Village Hall at 9.30? Starting then will allow extra time if the vans are late.

Questions 16–20

Now the third team will be the judges. For each of the various competitions we will have three judges. On the whole, they will have had experience of judging before. There will be a boat race, a swimming competition and the best fancy dress. A cash prize will be given to the winner in each category and for the two runners-up there will be book-tokens.

There is a sponsored mini-marathon and by the deadline lunch-time today we had 263 applicants with ages ranging from 15–60. That's 80 more than last year. Each entrant has paid a £20 registration fee to enter and all the profits will go to the local Children's Hospital to help fund much needed specialist apparatus.

The fourth team consists of the wardens for the day itself. We are expecting at least 10,000 people if last year is anything to go by. The fields near the entrance to the beach can be used as car parks and we need wardens to help make sure the actual parking is more organized than last year, which was a mess. We also need someone to be in charge of the first-aid, which will be at the entrance to the beach.

Finally, we need some volunteers for the clean-up. Last year we didn't do this very well and so the Council has agreed to provide large bags to collect all the recyclable material like glass and plastic etc., but we have to deal with the rest like left-over food ourselves. We don't want to leave piles of rotten food around or dangerous bottles.

TEST FOUR   Section 3

Questions 21–25

Adam: So what did you think of the practice exams last week?

Mary: You mean the mock exams?

Adam: Yeah. I thought some of them were tough.

Mary: They were certainly hard and generally they were very long.

Adam: Yeah. They were spread over a whole week, which made it impossible to relax.

Mary: Exactly. But what did you think of each test?

Adam: Of the seven exams we did, the least enjoyable for me were the two three-hour essay papers.

Mary: Why didn't you like the essay papers?

Adam: I am not particularly good at writing things down like that in a short space of time. And I don't think it's a good way of testing our theoretical knowledge of medicine.

Mary: I'm the opposite, I'm afraid. I'm much better in the written essay exams than the other types of tests. But what about the two multiple choice exam papers in basic science and anatomy?

Adam: They weren't too bad. If you didn't know the answer, all you had to do was guess.

Mary: Mmm. That's okay but I never feel comfortable with guessing. And you know that there is research that shows that women are disadvantaged when doing multiple-choice questions compared to men.

Adam: You have mentioned this before, but I am not sure I believe it.

Mary: It's true. Multiple-choice questions benefit men more than women. They are a male construct.

Adam: If you say so!

Mary: It's not if I say so. Anyway, you have to be careful with multiple-choice questions because of the negative marking. That can really bring the score down if you keep guessing and get all of the guesses wrong. It's double negative.

Adam: Yeah, that is a danger.

Mary: What about the role-play? Did you like that?

Adam: Yeah, with the actors and actresses as simulated patients. Yeah, I thought that was by far the best part of the exam.

Mary: Why was that?

Adam: What I liked about it was during the 24 test stations, we had a chance to show what we know about communicating with patients and show our practical medical knowledge etc.

Mary: Yes. I think I agree with you there. I enjoyed all of the stations, but I can tell you I was tired at the end. I have done a practice exam with 12 test stations, but not 24. It was exhausting, but also exhilarating.

Adam: I agree completely. It lasted nearly four hours in total with the break.

Questions 26–30

Adam: What did you think of the other two exams?

Mary: The two problem-solving tests? Mmm … I didn't think I was going to handle them very well, but in the end I think they went better than I thought they would. What I liked most was the test where we had to work in groups of four and to solve a problem we had to prioritize actions.

Adam: That was very interesting! I am not sure I did very well in that, though. Did you feel comfortable being in a group of four and having four examiners watching you as you discussed the problem?

Mary: We did practise it several times before. You learn to forget that someone is watching you.

Adam: But some people are better at speaking in group situations like that and they get the best marks.

Mary: The test doesn't just assess whether people can talk a lot. It's about showing you can listen, organize your thoughts and then show you can be part of a team, allowing other people to speak.

Adam: Well, we'll have to see how it goes. When do the results of the mocks come out?

Mary: They said next week. And then it's the Finals two weeks later.

Adam: Yeah, we've got that to look forward to. What is the policy on re-sits?

Mary: Why? Are you planning to fail?

Adam: No, but …. well, you know what I mean.

Mary: The re-sits are held in September and if there is any problem after that, it goes to appeal.

Adam: We'll just have to make sure we don't fail any part of the whole examination. I certainly wouldn't want to do any of it again.

Mary: Me neither. It's hard when you are not allowed to fail any of the exams.

Adam: I bet they don't have that policy in any other subject.

Mary: Probably not.

TEST FOUR   Section 4

Questions 31–35

In this the first lecture in our series on the changing face of the oceans of the world, we are going to look at the Indian Ocean, into which the Oceanography Department at the Institute here in Australia has been doing pioneering research over the past five years.

Let us start with some facts about the Indian Ocean to give you an idea of the scope and complexity of the enterprise we have undertaken. As you can see from the diagrams here on the screen showing the relative size of the planet's five oceans, the Indian Ocean comes third after the Pacific and Atlantic Oceans, but is larger than the Southern Ocean and the Arctic Ocean.

On this slide you can see that the Indian Ocean is different from the two larger oceans in that it is landlocked to the north and does not extend into the cold regions of the North Pole. Covering some 73,440,000 sq km, the ocean constitutes approximately one-seventh of the earth's surface and about 20 percent of the world's total ocean area. At the equator it is around 6,400 km wide with the average depth being about 3,400 metres and with the deepest point being the Java Trench at 7,450 metres.

Flowing into the Indian Ocean we have some of the world's greatest rivers: the Zambezi here, the Ganges here, the Indus, The Bhrahmaputra and the Tigris-Euphrates just here.

The two largest islands in the Indian Ocean, Madagascar, here off the coast of Africa and Sri Lanka, here off the southern tip of India, are structurally parts of the continents of Africa and Asia, while islands like the Seychelles are exposed tops of submerged ridges. The Maldives are low coral islands and Mauritius and Reunion are volcanic cones.

The surface waters of the ocean are warm, except where the ocean touches the cold waters to the south. A network of scientists, mainly oceanographers and meteorologists, from around the world, are monitoring changes in the ocean's temperature and acidity, especially where it meets the Southern Ocean, in order to see how global warming is having an effect on the waters there. An assessment is also being carried out on how this is impacting on low-lying habitats and peoples in the more populated coastal regions around the rim of the ocean. In the warmer north, islands are vulnerable to even the subtlest changes in sea levels and tides, so they are being closely watched. Moreover, a close eye is being kept on wind changes, especially alterations to the monsoon rains, typhoons, cyclones and any other natural phenomena.

Questions 36–40

In addition to the information sent from the ship that we have stationed off Antarctica in the south of the Indian Ocean, data are being transmitted round the clock from buoys anchored at various points around the Ocean. Five of these buoys are observing ice packs and icebergs coming into the Indian Ocean from Antarctica. Besides the buoys, data on cloud cover and wind and temperature change are received by satellite. Satellite images are also being used to record the size of the icebergs from the moment they break off from Antarctica. Their course is then mapped as they move out into the Southern Ocean.

Here at the Institute, the raw data from the various sources are received and the information is then constantly processed by a bank of computers. Once the data have been collated, the next step in the process is the analysis by experts here and at centres around the world, looking for even the slightest shift in patterns of temperature, wind and sea levels. In the light of the fact that this is a global enterprise, the institute is staffed 24 hours a day with researchers working in shifts and we are in constant contact with centres all around the world. In total, 900 experts from around the globe are involved in the programme.

The work at the Institute is now into the fifth year of a ten-year data collection, which began in …

UNIVERSITY of CAMBRIDGE
ESOL Examinations

The British Council

Education Australia
IELTS Australia

PENCIL must be used to complete this sheet

Centre number:

Please write your name below,

then write your four digit Candidate number in the boxes and shade the number in the grid on the right in PENCIL.

0 1 2 3 4 5 6 7 8 9
0 1 2 3 4 5 6 7 8 9
0 1 2 3 4 5 6 7 8 9
0 1 2 3 4 5 6 7 8 9

Test date (shade ONE box for the day, ONE box for the month and ONE box for the year):

Day: 01 02 03 04 05 06 07 08 09 10 11 12 13 14 15 16 17 18 19 20 21 22 23 24 25 26 27 28 29 30 31

Month: 01 02 03 04 05 06 07 08 09 10 11 12   Last digit of the **Year:** 0 1 2 3 4 5 6 7 8 9

IELTS Listening Answer Sheet

Version number:
Please enter the number in the boxes (one digit per line, starting at the top) and shade the number in the grid beside the box.

0 1 2 3 4 5 6 7 8 9
0 1 2 3 4 5 6 7 8 9
0 1 2 3 4 5 6 7 8 9
0 1 2 3 4 5 6 7 8 9
0 1 2 3 4 5 6 7 8 9

1	✓ 1 ✗	19	✓ 19 ✗
2	2	20	20
3	3	21	21
4	4	22	22
5	5	23	23
6	6	24	24
7	7	25	25
8	8	26	26
9	9	27	27
10	10	28	28
11	11	29	29
12	12	30	30
13	13	31	31
14	14	32	32
15	15	33	33
16	16	34	34
17	17	35	35
18	18	36	36
		37	37
		38	38
		39	39
		40	40

SAMPLE

| Marker's Initials | | Band Score | | Listening Total | |

IELTS L-R v5

DP452/352

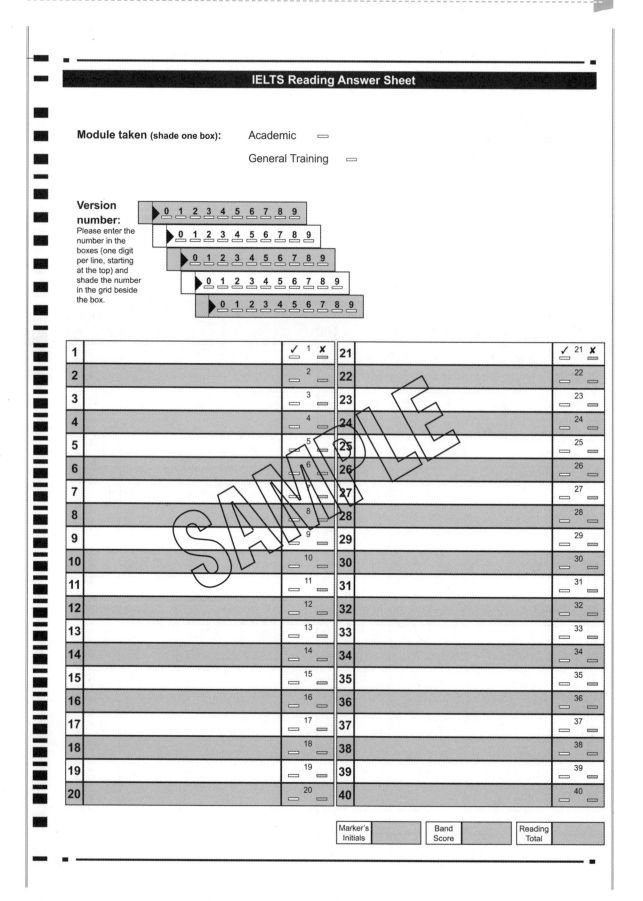

IELTS Reading Answer Sheet

Module taken (shade one box):   Academic   ▭

General Training   ▭

Version number:
Please enter the number in the boxes (one digit per line, starting at the top) and shade the number in the grid beside the box.

▶ 0 1 2 3 4 5 6 7 8 9
▶ 0 1 2 3 4 5 6 7 8 9
▶ 0 1 2 3 4 5 6 7 8 9
▶ 0 1 2 3 4 5 6 7 8 9
▶ 0 1 2 3 4 5 6 7 8 9

1		✓ 1 ✗	21		✓ 21 ✗
2		2	22		22
3		3	23		23
4		4	24		24
5		5	25		25
6		6	26		26
7		7	27		27
8		8	28		28
9		9	29		29
10		10	30		30
11		11	31		31
12		12	32		32
13		13	33		33
14		14	34		34
15		15	35		35
16		16	36		36
17		17	37		37
18		18	38		38
19		19	39		39
20		20	40		40

Marker's Initials		Band Score		Reading Total	

Reproduced by permission of University of Cambridge Local Examinations Syndicate.

IELTS Results

After you have completed the IELTS test, you will receive a Test Report Form which details your score. For each module of the test (Listening, Reading, Writing and Speaking) you will receive a Band Score of whole or half numbers between 0 and 9. These individual module scores are then added together and averaged for an Overall Band Score reported as a whole band or a half band (e.g. 6.5). The table below gives a summary fo the English of a candidage classified at each band level.

An IELTS Overall Band Score fo 6.0 or 6.5 is usually required for entry to universities and colleges in Australia, New Zealand, Canada and the United Kingdom. However, some institutions may ask for a higher socre.

Band 9 – expert user

Has fully operational command of the language: appropriate, accurate and fluent with complete understanding.

Band 8 – very good user

Has fully operational command of the language with only occasional unsystematic inaccuracies and inappropriacies. Misunderstandings may occur in unfamiliar situations. Handles complex detailed argumentation well.

Band 7 – good user

Has operational command of the language, though with occasional inaccuracies, inappropriacies and misunderstandings in some situations. Generally handles complex language well and understands detailed reasoning.

Band 6 – competent user

Has generally effective command of the language despite some inaccuracies, inappropriacies and misunderstandings. Can use and understand fairly complex language, particularly in familiar situations.

Band 5 – modest user

Has partial command of the language, coping with overall meaning in most situations, though is likely to make many mistakes. Should be able to handle basic communication in own field.

Band 4 – limited user

Basic competence is limited to familiar situations. Has frequent problems in understanding and expression. Is not able to use complex language.

Band 3 – extremely limited user

Conveys and understands only general meaning in very familiar situations. Frequent breakdowns in communication occur.

Band 2 – intermittent user

No real communication is possible except for the most basic information using isolated words or short formulae in familiar situations and to meet immediate needs. Has great difficulty in understanding spoken and written English.

Band 1 – non user

Essentially has no ability to use the language beyond possibly a few isolated words.

Band 0 – did not attempt the test

No assessable information provided.

Reproduced by permission of University of Cambridge Local Examinations Syndicate.

CD ONE

TRACK	TEST ONE

1   Test instructions

2   **Section 1**
Instructions
Questions 1–4
Instructions
Questions 5–10
End of section instructions

3   **Section 2**
Instructions
Questions 11–13
Instructions
Questions 14–20
End of section instructions

4   **Section 3**
Instructions
Questions 21–25
Instructions
Questions 26–30
End of section instructions

5   **Section 4**
Instructions
Questions 31–40
End of test instructions

TEST TWO

6   Test intructions

7   **Section 1**
Instructions
Questions 1–4
Instructions
Questions 5–10
End of section instructions

8   **Section 2**
Instructions
Questions 11–13
Instructions
Questions 14–20
End of section instructions

9   **Section 3**
Instructions
Questions 21–23
Instructions
Questions 24–30
End of section instructions

10   **Section 4**
Instructions
Questions 31–40
End of test instructions

CD TWO

TRACK	TEST THREE

1   Test instructions

2   **Section 1**
Instructions
Questions 1–5
Instructions
Questions 6–10
End of section instructions

3   **Section 2**
Instructions
Questions 11–13
Instructions
Questions 14–20
End of section instructions

4   **Section 3**
Instructions
Questions 21–26
Instructions
Questions 27–30
End of section instructions

5   **Section 4**
Instructions
Questions 31–40
End of test instructions

TEST FOUR

6   Test instructions

7   **Section 1**
Instructions
Questions 1–4
Instructions
Questions 5–10
End of section instructions

8   **Section 2**
Instructions
Questions 11–15
Instructions
Questions 16–20
End of section instructions

9   **Section 3**
Instructions
Questions 21–25
Instructions
Questions 26–30
End of section instructions

10   **Section 4**
Instructions
Questions 31–40
End of test instructions